T0116849

Return to Muddy Brook

A. W. Dawson

Trafford rev. 10/12/2011

 www.trafford.com

North America & international
toll-free: 1 888 232 4444 (USA & Canada)
phone: 250 383 6864 ♦ fax: 812 355 4082

To MOM

[my bestes pal]

Like Bob Hope use to sing,
THANKS FOR THE MEMORIES.

This book is a story about a family, two young boys, a father, and the main character , a mother, her life and the boys lives and the way they were brought up, and where they grew up. The period of time was during the 1940s and 50s.

The town they came from that molded their lives, the people that influenced them through the years, and their mother, the rock of the family that withstood intimidation from in-laws, and alcoholic brothers that relied on her to take care of them through the years. Her father, that had to be looked after in his late years. The woman that stayed in an almost loveless marriage for the sake of her two sons, who she loved more than life, and for her GOD that gave her the strength to endure the hardships of life.

The street where the family grew, the friends that they made, and in the town that they loved and kept coming back to, throughout the years.

CHAPTER 1

Where to begin my story? I guess the best place would be at the beginning. At sixty nine years old, it's a task to try to remember all the facts of the 1940's and 1950's. These were good and bad years to grow up in Muddy Brook, or better known as Pearl River, in New York State. During these early years of my life, in nineteen hundred and forty one, the year that I was born, we lived in Bardonia. NY. When I was in my second year, age two, we moved to this small town.

I was the younger of two children. My brother was born in 1935 and was six years older than me. When I was born, he had already started school and was going into the first grade. It was a big step for my mother and father to make this move, it was just a short time after the attack on Pearl Harbor and our country was at war.

Born in 1907, in Spring Valley, NY, my father grew up with his three other brothers, all of which had obligations to the family, all the boys had to go to work at an early age. Their father, my grandfather was killed working for the Erie Lackawanna Rail Road, when my Dad was nine years old. He fell from the train at his home stop and was killed. At this time the four sons had to quit school at an early age. The oldest son Bill went to work for the same railroad where his father was killed and stayed there for forty three years. He married his wife, Emma and raised two beautiful girls and lived in Elisibeth, NJ until his death.

My Uncle George, the second oldest son, left school at fifteen and became a carpenters apprentice and stayed at that profession his whole life and became a cabinet maker and a finish carpenter. He married for a short time, which did not work out, divorced and lived the rest of his life in the house he grew up in that the family owned for over sixty years. He had no children of his own and I think that he loved his two nephews, my brother and me as his own sons. He was a great guy.

My Uncle Rob, the third son was a sickly young man. He did not go out to work, when his father got killed, he was too frail and weak and was bedridden most of his life. His mother took special care of him and when she passed on Uncle George took over the task of taking care of Uncle Rob until he passed on while in his mid thirties.

Uncle Rob passed away in 1947 and was the first of the brothers to pass away, two years after his mother died in

1945. His brother George took care of him at the homestead until he died of tuberculosis. I think that he lost the will to live when his mother passed and he went down hill shortly after.

Uncle Bill was the next to pass on in 1951 from a heart attack and left his wife, Emma and two young daughters, Doris and Gladis, both if which grew up in Elisibeth, NJ. Far away from Spring Valley, NY...

As I remember, we didn't see much of that part of the family, and that was too bad, but the girls grew up just fine and had children of their own. Their mother Emma passed away in 2001 and is buried in the family plot at New Hempstead Cemetery, just a short ways from Spring Valley. She lays to rest, next to her beloved husband Bill Dawson.

Back in the early twenty's, my grandmother had the foresight to buy the family burial plot at New Hempstead Cemetery for the large sum of about four dollars a grave and she bought ten grave sights on the same plot, which at today's prices would be worth about three thousand a grave or about thirty thousand dollars for the whole plot. She did this when my grandfather John Dawson was killed in 1921 on the railroad. She also lies to rest there next to her husband John, her sons, Rob, Bill and George who passed in 1955, and my father Frank M. Dawson Sr., who died in 1975.

Also buried in the plot is my mother, Anna M. Dawson who died in 1984 and is next to her husband Frank. My grandmother Elsie Runge who passed away in 1937 is there also.

I will go there as well, but not yet, I hope. My brother Frank Jr. also, if he so desires.

Being only four years old in 1945 I don't remember Grandma Dawson that well. My brother, Frank would remember her better than me being he is six years older than me. This is the year that she passed away. I remember that she was a harsh woman, very strict and set in her ways. She had to be tough, her husband had dies in 1921 and she had four sons to bring up and one of them was very sickly.

Three of the sons had to get jobs, of any kind, to help support the family and the house. George went to work as a carpenter's helper, Bill was given a job on the railroad and my father got a job in a butcher shop in town, sweeping floors and making deliveries of meat to homes and whatever else he had to do to make some money for his mother. He only went to the eleventh grade in high school, he had to leave school and get a full time job to help pay the expenses of the homestead.

This was the early twenty's and at sixteen years old, he became a plumber's helper and was glad to find this work. It was just before the great depression and there weren't that many jobs to be had. He was a hard worker who like his job and found his nitch in life.

In the early thirty's, he went on a blind date with my mother, Anna Runge. She was a small petite woman, only five foot tall and about one hundred ten pounds. He was smitten right off the start and this was the beginning of the end of Frank Dawson as a single man.

I remember my father as always working. He was doing something all the time. This must have been the same, before he met mom. After he met her, he was having trouble thinking straight and didn't know what to do. Dad was real shy, never had a girl friend before and these feelings were brand new to him and this was lousing his head up completely. If he was going to court my mother, he was going to have to slow down on his work habits, and make time to see her, before she got away.

CHAPTER 2

I'm getting ahead of myself, so let's go back to before my father and his brothers were born to 1842 when Spring Valley was known as Pascack and a small area was called Scotland, after a lot of the immigrants that settled there. The name of the town was changed to Spring Valley when some original settlers noticed a fresh water spring, feeding a large pond in the lower part of the town. Hence the name changes.

There were other small towns sprouting fourth around this time of the century, close to Spring Valley, there was an area called Pamona, to the north, Nanuet and West Nyack, to the south, and then there was Muddy Brook, a small hamlet, south east ,about seven miles from the new named town of Spring Valley. The main thing that put the Valley as we called the town, on the map was the Lackawanna Rail Road, which in them days was the main source of transportation to Hoboken New Jersey, where ferry boats would take people to New York City across the Hudson River. The commuter trains left the Valley early in the morning and return up till nine o'clock at night. A lot of people worked in the city and the trains ran through the small towns like Nanuet and Muddy Brook, and small Jersey towns on the way to the ferries. This is where Grandpa Dawson worked, the railroad and shortly getting that job, he met and married Mary Wood, my grandmother around the 1890s.

In 1892, Uncle Bill was born, followed by Rob in 1896 and my Uncle George born in 1902, which was the year that Spring Valley became an incorporated village. My father, the baby of the family was born in 1907 and was the last child Mary Dawson was to have.

Shortly after John and Mary Dawson married, they bought their first and only house, which was on Myrtle Avenue. That's where they raised their four sons. The home was close to the Erie Railroad tracks and station where Grandpa would go to work each day. Myrtle Avenue was a dirt road, as most of the roads in Spring Valley were and only a few blocks from town, easy for shopping and other transportation if needed. It wasn't a bad time for the Dawson boys to grow up and they were all busy with school and other things, like helping around the house for their mother and father. John Dawson was a stern man, not brutal, but strong willed and sometimes hard on the boys through the years. I think he wanted them

7

to have the schooling that he did not have and wanted to make sure none of them got into any real trouble with the law or any other kind. He wanted to make sure they finished school and had every advantage they could have to make a good living for themselves. Unfortunately this was not to pass. When he was killed on the job at the railroad in 1921, Bill and George had to leave school to get jobs to bring money into the home. Uncle Rob left school also, but could not work because he was sickly, weak and frail. My dad stayed in school until the eleventh grade and then went to work

Dad was doing well, in school before he had to leave .He was on the baseball team, as a catcher, and wasn't a bad hitter either. After practice he would go right home, to help his mother around the house and run errands. The first job he had when he left school was in a butcher shop, sweeping the floors and empting the excess barrels of fat and lard that would get full during the day. His boss liked him and would give him special prices on meat. He knew that the family had lost the main bread winner when John Dawson was killed. The Dawson boys were well known in Spring Valley, and well liked also.

Mary Dawson was a good woman and mother. She was strong willed like her husband and very firm, when it came to raising her four sons. They would all have obligations towards the house. Robert, of course could not work, he was week and was house bound at the homestead. He never left. This took its toll on her, mentally and physically. It was a blessing that she had the other three healthy boys, able to work and to support the home. George was the one son that helped her the most, taking care of Rob, and stayed home most of the time, when he wasn't working. Bill was away from the house a lot of the time, working and Dad and George had to pick up the slack. My father left the butcher shop and took a job as a plumber's helper and that was the start of his final career. That was the best move, at that time, he could have ever made.

Back in 1841, there was a small hamlet four miles to the south east called Nannawitts Meadow, named after a Kakiat Indian, named Nannawitt who settled there. In 1856 the name of the hamlet was changed to Nanuet New York and remains that way today.

The Erie Railroad started service through this town in 1869 and it was known as The Pascack Line and ran through Nanuet, south towards Muddy Brook, and on into New Jersey. For the neighboring areas such as West Nyack and Bardonia, New York, This was good and many people utilized the rail to get to work. One of the first buildings constructed in this town was a railroad station building. Travel in these times was difficult, all the roads were dirt, full of pot holes and getting from place to place was either walk, or horse and wagon. Needless to say this method took a long time, but you did what you had to do. Close to the turn of the century the invention of the automobile made it somewhat easier to say the least. This town was located in the township or area known as Clarkstown, all part of Rockland County, New York. Travel to Spring Valley, four miles away or to Muddy Brook, two miles to the south was not that hard. This could be walked or done by horseback or horse and wagon, which ever was available to you at the time.

Muddy Brook was another small hamlet in 1841 with some small bordering areas such as Naurashaun after the Indians that settled there and Orangeburg, New York. The small town was nothing much to speak of in those days. A fellow named Julius Brauensdorff came here in the late 1860s, bought up a lot of property, which was pretty cheap back then because most of it was wet lands, with a small river or brook running through the middle of the land. Julius did a lot of planning for his property during those years and in 1869 when the railroad came through his land, it was time for bigger and better things to happen to Muddy Brook.

In 1872 a young doctor came to town and was working around some property he had bought along the small brook of which the town was named. He noticed something in the water and bent down to get a better look and found that there were some mussels in the stream. He picked about a half a dozen out of the water and opened them all and most of them were empty, but two of them contained small pearls. His name was Dr. Ves Bogert. In that year, that was the end of Muddy Brook and the new name of the town was changed to Pearl River, New York.

Pearl River was a border town with Mountvale, New Jersey and being a border town there was a lot of wagon traffic between the two states. This small town was only two miles south on the main dirt road or by railroad.

Another area close to Pearl River was Blauvelt, New York, about five miles east of town. After the town was renamed Mr. Braunsdorf started to plan out the roads of the town, of which was on most of his land. He made the main thoroughfare Central Avenue and two streets parallel to that were Washington Avenue on the north side and Franklin Avenue on the south side. Main Street ran across all three streets, he named the streets after President Washington and Ben Franklin, both men whom he admired greatly. Mr. Braunsdorf became known as the Father of Pearl River and rightfully so.

He also built a factory in town that built sewing machines about the late 1880s or so. He was an inventor of some of the machines the factory turned out. It also produced some kinds of printing machines. The business grew rapidly and employed most of the people that moved to his town of Pearl River. Buildings were going up rapidly in town and new homes were being built and new streets were being made all over the town. His company was called the Aetna Sewing Machine Company and later on in years became the Dexter Folder Company. This factory and these companies employed many of the residents of the town. It was located on Central Avenue just over the train tracks and it had its own railroad siding for shipping and receiving materials for the factory. Mr. Braunsdorf was no dummy and planned everything out for his town very well.

While Mr. Braunsdorf was busy with his factories and helping to lay out more of the town a young man named Ernest Lederle came to the area north of town towards Nanuet and bough a large parcel of land to build his pharmaceutical plant. He also wanted to take advantage of the railroad for shipping and getting supplies. The plant started to be built in 1906 and when finished at the point they wanted at that time, hired many people from both Pearl River and Nanuet to work there. Towns grew very fast, housing boomed, schools had to be built and food stores had to supply the many people that were coming into this area. Things were going well for both towns; it was too good to be true. The railroad station was built in town as well as many other buildings which still stand today.

Times were good until the early 1914's; the First World War started and many of our young men went in the different armed forces. They went to fight and die for their wonderful country, the United States of America. This was to be the war to end all wars and it ended in 1918. We lost many fine men and woman. Lederle Laboratories made a lot of plasma and medicine for the war and was working overtime to keep up with the demand. After the war was over, over there, like George M Cohen sang, the Yankee Doodle Dandy's were coming home. The returning veterans needed care and jobs to support their families and get the country back in shape.

CHAPTER 4

Now that I have talked about the Spring Valley side of the family, the Dawson side, let's talk about Mom side, the Runge side. My Grandfather, William Runge Sr., was born in a small town outside Hamburg, Germany in 1872. Not much is known about his early life except that he came to America by ship, in 1887, when he was fifteen years old. His family was poor in Germany and he did not have that much schooling and went to work in the town's small brewery and worked with the brew meister there at the age of twelve. He was a good worker and learned the art of brewing fairly well. The land of golden opportunity was calling him and with his meager savings he caught a ship to New York City.

He landed at Ellis Island with hundreds of other passengers and went through the many lines to become admitted to the new world he had heard so much about. On the voyage over, he contracted a raspy cough and when he arrived at Ellis, people there held him over and quarantined him for three days. They though he had whooping cough. He became scared and afraid that they would send him back to Germany and not let him enter the land of his dreams. They finally cleared him and he landed on the shores of lower Manhattan.

Not knowing much English he was very nervous the first few days in the new land. The only job he knew was brewing beer and he thought he would try to get that kind of work. There was not that kind of work to be had at that time. Most of the breweries were located in Brooklyn, another borough of the city and he did not know of this fact, and wouldn't know how to get there if he did. He had a little money left and he found a boarding house, which gave him a room and at least a roof over his head. Being only fifteen years old, he had a tough time finding a job.

One of his new found friends, also in the same boat as he was, out of work, told him that the hotels close by in Manhattan, were hiring bus boys and bell hops. He was close by so he and his friend went over to the Waldorf Astoria Hotel, applied for work and were hired on the spot. His friend became a bellhop and a busboy in the dining room and Grand pop William became a dishwasher and also a busboy. This was good, for he was about to run out of money and they could eat some of the leftovers they had in the big kitchen. Like I said he was a hard worker something he learned how to do in Germany and worked his way up the ladder. People liked him and after a year or so he became a waiter. Many of the steady patrons of the hotel would ask for him to wait on them. He was building up quite a reputation in the dining room and the hotel. This was good and he liked his job very much and became very proficient at it.

He stayed there many years and after a while he met a chamber maid at the hotel, her name was Elsie, short for Elisabeth and they started to court, back then that's what they called dating. She also was a hard worker and a very good looking young woman about nineteen years old. After a short dating period, six months or a little more, they married and moved up to the Bronx and got a small one bedroom apartment. She was now Mrs. William Runge and was very happy for a while.

My Grandfather started drinking, not much at first but as time went on it became more visible that it was getting heavier. By the time six months had passed, Elsie was pregnant with their first son, William, who later on in life they called Whitey because he was so fair and his hair was very blond, almost white. When whitey was born, Grandma left her job at the hotel and began to take in washing as so many did in the early 1900's. Sixteen months after her first son was born she delivered another son, Albert and two years later another boy came along. He had a nickname that stuck, Giggy and that's what we called him all through his life. Elsie was a great Mother, she tolerated a lot of grief from her husband through this period, his drinking became heavier and he would come home from the Waldorf pretty well blitzed. She took in sewing as well as washing and became a very good seamstress. She had three boys, all young growing up in the big city and she loved her husband very much, so she put up with lot of "Pops" crap.

A few years after Giggy was born, in May 1909 my Mother was born into the Runge family. Anna Marie Runge, a very pretty baby as my Grandmother would always brag. Before she came along, the family had moved to a much bigger apartment, not far away from the first one, still on Tremont Avenue, still in the Bronx. It was a nice neighborhood and it was easy for Pop to take the trolley car down to work at the hotel. After working there for many years he became the head waiter in the main dining room and was well respected. Needless to say Pop did not drink on the job. He would not put his livelihood in jeopardy that way, knowing that he had a new baby girl to feed and take care of. While pregnant, Grandma wanted a girl so bad she had the three boys who were a handful and prayed for a baby girl she could pamper and play with as she grew, which she did.

She loved Anna Marie very much and the three boys would fuss over their sister all the time. Pop was not an overly loving person. He did not know how to show affection easily. In his own way, he loved Anna very much as he loved Elsie but had a lot of trouble showing it. The three boys on the other hand was a different story. With them he was hard and strict almost to the point of being a tyrant. It was New York City and it was rough on the streets and you had to be tough out there or you were going to get your ass kicked and they knew it. As the boys grew up they always loved and respected their Mother and baby Anna.

The three Runge boys did not feel the same way about their Father. They did not like the way Pop treated their Mother when he was drinking, he could be very nasty and belligerent towards her and the boys as well.

Growing up on the streets was taking its toll on the boys. Whitey was working but he was gambling also, nothing big, dice and cards. Albert was working as a mechanic in a car shop and in 1914 when the war to end all wars, World War One broke out; he enlisted in the U.S. Army and went to fight in Belgium. He was wounded and received a Purple Heart metal. He was in the artillery pulling the cannons with mules and while taking care of this one mule, which did not like Uncle Al, the mule kicked him in the ass and broke his hip and that's how he got the Purple Heart. True story and the whole family would laugh about it. Al didn't think it was too funny because he was shipped home by Red Cross Ship, covered in plaster from the waist to his foot. He was done with the war and received a veteran's pension from Uncle Sam, the rest of his life and the Army buried him when he died. He got out of the hospital before the war was over and the hip never healed or felt the same. He always cursed that mule.

Giggy on the other hand had a lot of his Father in him because of bad ear infections when he was a child and it left him with almost no hearing in his left ear, this meant that he could not go to war and fight as Al did and was classified

4F. It didn't stop him from fighting at home in the streets. He was quick with his hands and could scrap with the best of men.

He had a reputation on the streets of being a tough guy and nobody to fool with. Uncle Whitey and Al used to get into it with him and Grandma had to tell them to behave themselves even while they were almost full grown. She was the boss and that was that. God forbid anybody went against their Mother or Anna, their baby sister. Even Pop had to watch himself, for the boys were grown now and they wouldn't tolerate him giving their Mom or little Sister any shit when he was drunk.

Pop had a lot of friends and connections at the Waldorf Astoria and he knew the ins and outs of a lot of things. He knew where people could go to have a good time, get tickets to all the shows on Broadway, and sporting events, baseball games and prize fights. He had the ways and means to get the so called big shots what they wanted and needed. He knew Lillian Russell and the Ziegfield Follies and J. P. Morgan, the banker and some of the Rockefeller family. This was the roaring twenty's and the whole city and the country was one big party. The big war was over and everybody was making a buck. Where ever and whatever they had to do to make it. Then the bottom fell out of everything, the Stock Market crashed in 1928 and the whole country went belly up. Big investors lost millions, businesses went bankrupt and there were banks in big trouble. People that had savings in banks lost everything, work in the country stopped and the bread lines were all over the city. Times were hard and I mean hard.

With the big crash, company CEO's were jumping out of windows of big office buildings on Wall Street, investors following them and a lot of people depressed were blowing their brains out, the whole country went broke overnight. If that wasn't bad enough there was Prohibition put into effect in 1920 and ended in 1922 when Franklin D. Roosevelt ended it. During this time period there were speakeasy's illegal clubs and bars where people could get booze and beer and party the night away.

Prohibition did not hurt the three Runge brothers, to the contrary, Uncle Whitey was in the girl business, the big girl business and I think they called it prostitution. He knew where to get girls for parties for the right people and brother Giggy was running illegal whiskey for the same parties and Uncle al was the driver that delivered the girls and the booze to this many affairs all around the city, even to the Waldorf where their Father worked. Pop even set up some of the parties for his most important and rich people that he had served in the hotel dining room.

They had quite a good thing going on and they made a lot of money and of course, Mama and little Anna, knew nothing of what was going on. By this time Anna was almost finished with school and she had a part time job as an operator in the phone company and was helping Mama with the laundry. Mama always had a clean pressed white shirt for Pop to go to work at the hotel.

CHAPTER 5

It's a good thing mama new nothing of what the boys were doing, she would not approve at all. I think my mother knew and she was sworn to secrecy, not to tell mama a thing. Things were going well and the secret was kept until Uncle Giggy got caught with a load of boot leg whiskey and during a scuffle that pursued, he shot a government agent with a 22 pistol. He was arrested and was convicted and sentenced to one year in Ossining Prison, north of the city. Thank GOD that the agent didn't die and was only shot in the leg.

By this time in my mother's life, all the brothers were out on their own and living in different parts of MANHATTAN. Whitey was living in the Inwood section of upper northern Manhattan and Al and Giggy moved down on LENOX

AVE. around 140th street near the HARLEM section of the city. The subways made it easy for the boys to see each other and their mother, pop and their sister, still on TREMONT AVE.

1929 was just around the corner and folks were trying to get over the big bust up on Wall ST. The winter months in the city were harsh and the bread lines were long. The spring could not come fast enough for my mother. When it turned warmer, mama and Anna would go up to BARDONIA NY. by train, to see mama's aunt and her daughter, Alviena, who lived on a small farm close to Nanuet. Anna and Alviena were about the same age, as was another cousin Irma. All the three girls were in their early twenties and all three were very pretty, Anna was the cutest of the three, and the smallest. Alviena and Irma both worked at LEDERLE LABRATORIES, between the two towns of Nanuet and Pearl River.

Anna would go up to see her two cousins a lot that summer. It was only a one day trip, about seventeen miles by train and she could come back to the Bronx later in the evening. Sometimes she would stay overnight and spend the week end. Alveina had met this young man that worked in the plumbing shop at LEDERLE, and wanted to set up a blind date with him and Anna. She didn't want anything to do with a blind date and that was that. After two or three weeks of saying no, my mother went out on the date with this plumber's helper, FRANK DAWSON. According to my mother, they didn't hit it off right away. She said that he was shy and fumbled over himself most of the first date. He wouldn't even try to hold her hand and she only got a hand shake, no kiss, when they said good night. She was not impressed, but she thought that he was really good looking and his shyness was cute. She told Alveina that she would go out with Frank again, and she would take care of the shyness problem on her own. After all, she did come from the city and had dated boys before, and she liked him a lot, but didn't want to rush into anything too fast.

My Father still lived at home with his Mother and two other Brothers Rob and George. He took the job at Lederle Labs after working for a plumber in Spring Valley for about a year. It was a good change for him; the train ran through the Lederle property into Pearl River. The plant was only about four miles from home. This is where he met Alviena, who ended up playing cupid for him and Mom. Mom would come up from Tremont Avenue, stay at the farm with Alviena and they would double date with her new boyfriend Rudy. He was a great guy and worked for the Federal Government. He had some connections in NY and Mama Runge asked him if he could help to get Uncle Giggy out of Sing Sing in Ossining. He was able to help and got his sentenced reduced down to three months from a one year term and they release Giggy from jail. When he was released, he told his Mother that he was out of the boot leg whisky business for good. He went back to Lenox Avenue and got his old room back close to his Brother Al.

Rudy and Alviena got married and setup housekeeping on the farm at Bardonia. After dating Frank for close to a year Mom told him that she was getting tired of coming up from the city. They finally decided to get married and set the date. Dad went home and told his Mother that he was going to marry Anna, whom she had met once or twice. She was not happy about the news.

Frank had told his older brother, George, about Anna and him getting married, and that the date was set. George liked her, but warned him that his mother will hit the moon when she hears of the plans. She did, and she and her youngest son got into a hell of an argument over the wedding. She told him that she thought that ANNA was a fast woman, a city slicker, and that she wasn't the kind of girl that she wanted in the Dawson family, and she wouldn't allow it.

Well Uncle George didn't want to go against his mother at the time because he and Rob were still living at the homestead a long with Frank and like I said before, she was the boss of the house, and that was that. My father was intimidated by his mother to a point and let the argument rest and left the house and drove to Bardonia, to see his girlfriend. When he told my mother, about the words that he had with his mother, and the things that she had said, mom got upset that she felt that way after only meeting her a few times. She was insulted and she told my father, that in no uncertain terms how she felt. Being full blooded of German decent, she did not walk away from insults like this easily. Her pride and her dignity were hurt and she was not the kind of woman, Mary Dawson, made her out to be and she was not.

She informed dad that if he wanted to marry her, it was time that he stood up to his mother and let her know how things were going to be with them. They were getting married and that was it. It was Sunday and mom had to get back to the city. She had to go to work the next day, as did Frank. He would drive her back. He had bought a used 1917 HUDSON, PHAETON, 6 cylinders convertible and it being only twelve years old was in very good shape. It was kept in good condition and he took good care of it. They did not speak much on the trip to the BRONX; she had been hurt and did not know what was going to happen next. When they arrived at the apartment building on Tremont Ave, she got out of the car without kissing him goodbye, and told him that she needed some time to think about getting married. She needed to know if he was the man she had thought he was, or if he was going to be swayed by his mother. My mother wasn't going to take 2nd place to her new mother-in-law and that was that. Not after she had said those nasty things about her. She told Frank that she would not be going up to Bardonia the next week end and that she would call him later on in the week. They said good bye and she went up stairs to the apartment where her mother, Elsie was waiting. Of course she wasn't going to call him, and wanted him to stew in it for a while. After a week of not hearing from Anna, dad started to get nervous, he asked Alviena and Irma if they had heard from her, and of course they said no, which was a lie, the girls always talked during the week and they would fill mom in on what was going on with him and he had confided to

Irma that he missed her, missed talking to her on the phone and that she said that she would call, and didn't. He was starting to sweat and mom knew all about it, through her cousins. She was going to call him, but he beat her to it.

He wanted to see her, he said that they had to talk and that he loved her and didn't care what his mother thought and he wanted to be with her forever. He was hooked, her plan had worked so far and she was glad that he had called her first. The three girls started to make the wedding plans. Nothing too big, the small church and then a gathering of family and friends at the farm in Bardonia.

CHAPTER 6

The wedding was set. It was to take place in the small Lutheran Church, about a half mile from the farm. Mom and pop Runge, and all of mom's brothers came up from the city. Dad's brothers, George and Bill were there, but Grandma Dawson and Brother Rob did not attend. Robert was to sickly and weak and grandma just had her normal attitude towards the whole thing. She didn't like my mother and the feeling was the same. It was better all around that she stayed away.

They said that my mother looked beautiful, in her white and pink dress; her blond hair cut a little short, as it was worn back in those times and her skin was very fair. Dad stood around six ft. tall and was thin built, not skinny and a full head of blond hair and blue, grey eyes, he was a pretty good looking young man of twenty two years old. He looked very sharp in his new grey suite. The party afterwards went well, no one got smashed or out of line. The family from the city stayed over at the farm, there was plenty of room in this five bedroom farmhouse. Uncle Bill went home to ELISABETH NJ., to his family and George went home to Spring Valley.

During the wedding party at the farm, Gerhart met one of Aunt Irma's close friends and working companions, Miss Ava Schultz, a very pretty young woman and Giggy was smitten right off the bat. They continued to see each other and love was in the air. He didn't drive so he had to come up out of the city by train, she would meet him at the station in Pearl River and walk to her parents house not far from the train depot. He would stay over at the farm and return back to Lenox Avenue on Sunday evening.

The idea of Miss Schultz coming to visit him down in the city was out of the question. Lenox Avenue wasn't the type of place you wanted to bring a nice young woman. The bar where he worked as a bouncer and bartender was rough and the customers and drunks that hung out there were crude, abnockious and loud mouthed and I'm being polite saying these things. It wouldn't impress her at all. She finally came to the city, to Tremont Avenue only to meet Mama and Pop Runge. They loved her and things were going well. Her Mother and Father liked Giggy, too. Her Father was a drinker of sorts but not the kind of drinker that his future son in law was. He kept a low profile around the Schultz homestead. The relationship went on about five months and they got married in secret and waited to tell the whole family when they could find a nicer place to live than Lenox Avenue. They seemed to be happy at first, but Giggy started to drink very heavily and became mean to his wife.

He wouldn't beat her or be physical abusive to her, but the hollering and screaming, and coming home at all hours of the night, so drunk he could hardly stand up. She stayed with him almost three years and during that time she gave birth to a baby boy, Robert. Soon after he was born she started to make plans to leave Giggy and she had already discussed it with her parents. They wanted her to come home with Robby, as she called him, and one day she had had enough of his abuse and crap. She packed up her clothes and the baby's things and caught the train for Pearl River. As far as she was concerned the marriage was ended and she was keeping the baby with her and that was it. Her farther sent word down to Giggy, not to call, not to write and stay away and leave her alone or else. It was over and Giggy stayed away and moved back near his brother on LENOX Ave.

A few weeks before mom and dad got married, they had rented a small one bedroom bungalow right across from the church where the wedding to place. It was not very far away from the farm, about five blocks. The rooms were not that big but it was just fine for the both of them. Mom left her job in the city and Alveina got her a job at Lederlie working with her. It was coming up onto 1933 and there were problems in Europe. This little guy named Hitler was stirring up Germany, and making threats to other countries, and acting like a big shot, but he was not bothering the United States, yet.

Mom and dad were both working at Lederle, but dad was itching to make a move. He met a friend of his that just had gotten a job at a new mental hospital in Orangeburg NY, a few miles east of Pearl River. It was called Rockland State Hospital and the construction started in late 1927 when the broke ground and the first three buildings were still being completed and they needed skilled craftsman to work on the project. That was right up my dad's alley. By then he was almost a full qualified mechanic plumber and he was ready to make the move. He talked it over with mom and they decided to go for it. He was hired right away and the money was more the he had made at Lederle.

He started out working in the steam tunnels, installing steam pipes which would feed heat to the buildings. They were making a lot of tunnels because they planned to have about thirty buildings all toll and they all had to be heated. After the pipes were installed they were coated with asbestos covering to hold in the heat. Back then they didn't know how dangerous asbestos could be to your health and lungs. He also worked on the power house that was being built to produce the steam for the heat. This work was done in the winter months, so at least he was working all year around. Like I said before, Dad was a good and hard worker and well liked. They were both doing fine and would plan to go to see her mother and pop on the weekends.

It was a cold fall in 1934 and at Thanksgiving that year there was snow on the ground, not much just a heavy dusting. All the trees were bare and the pretty colored leaves were lying on the ground covered with a little snow. December was cold too, with heavier snow falling two days before Christmas Day. A white Christmas was just the right time for Mom to tell her husband that there was going to an addition to the family and he was going to become a Daddy. He was so happy and proud he went out and told everybody he saw. They had big New Years Eve party at the farm and brought 1935 in, in style.

The rest of the family in New York City were very happy about the news and Grandma Runge started to make plans and was ready to come up- to help her daughter when her time got close. Mom left work and stayed home around July for the rest of here term. She was a small built woman and the baby was getting bigger every day. He back was bothering her and she had a hard time standing for long periods of time. It was a hot summer that year and she prayed that the weather would get cooler. Elsie knew that Anna was having a hard time with her back, the heat and still trying to take care of my Dad, while he was still working two jobs to keep the bills paid. Dad helped Mom as much as he could, when he was home. He did the laundry and the food shopping and some cooking also. Elsie came to Bardonia to be with Mom, slept on the couch and took over the chores of the house.

The weather did not get any cooler and was in the 90's most of time in August and Mom had had it by then. She was ready to have this baby and make this back pain go away. Well she got her wish and on September 10, 1935 she delivered a baby boy, Franklyn Maural Dawson, Jr. Dad had his son and strutted around like a peacock. The baby was a good size, close to eight pounds, over twenty inches long and short blonde hair. Mom did not have an easy delivery, she being small and junior being as big as he was.

Grandma Runge stayed with Mom for about a month after Frankie was born. The little bungalow was getting smaller now with three adults and a baby. There was no room for a crib so the baby found that a dresser drawer would have to do for the time being. Dad told Mom that it was time to move on to bigger and better things and get a bigger house or apartment. This was a no-brainer and when Mom got stronger they went out looking for a bigger place to live. It took a while but they found a nice little house on a dirt road in Pearl River. They got help from Uncle George, Bill and some other friends and piled their things into a small old rack truck and moved into the first house they rented on Martin Place. What a nice quiet little street, it was only two blocks from Central Avenue and the main section of town. Franklin Avenue was the next block over to the North and the small Methodist Church was on the corner. It was a great find for Frankie and the family to grow.

CHAPTER 7

This was not the best of times to be starting a family. It was still known as the depression years and December of 1934 was a very bad time for the Runge family. Two days before Christmas Day they found Uncle Whitey, dead in his hotel room in upper Manhattan. He died of pneumonia and none of the family that that he was ill. Mom and Grandma went to Pop and hold him the bad news and of course, he broke down. His first born son had died and it took awhile for him to compose himself.

After a day or so the other sons told Pop that they needed to get a hold of $400 to have Whitey buried and that Anna and Frank would set the whole service up. Back in those days you could set the whole burial up through the cemetery. Mom had the good foresight to go to New Hempstead Cemetery and purchase a plot with four grave sites, well away from the Dawson plot and that's where they buried William Runge, Jr. (Uncle Whitey). Grandma Runge collapsed at the funeral, of all three sons, Whitey was her favorite one, the kindest and the most thoughtful and he always showed his love for her. No one ever told Grandma what Uncle Whitey did for a living. That remained a secret, forever. That was not a very Merry Christmas time and it was just after the New Year of 1935 that Mom found out that she was pregnant with Frankie.

The year of 1935 started off on the wrong foot. In February, a man named Bruno Hauptmann was convicted and sentenced to death for the kidnapping of the Charles Lindbergh baby. On September8, two days before Frankie was born Hughy Long, the U. S. Senator from Louisiana was shot and killed. That was big news, except that Adolf Hitler was invading more of the small countries in Europe and it looked like he wanted to be king of the world.

It was a good thing that Dad had a steady job at the new mental hospital, with the new baby and moving to Pearl River. The power house at the hospital was almost fully built and ready to go on line and produce steam heat for the Administration building and the first of the other three being built, Male Reception in which would house the first of sixty male mental patients. New staff was being hired and trained. More buildings were being built, more tunnels dug and more steam pipes installed. The tunnel work had its draw backs. In the winter months when it was cold, a lot of rats would come into the tunnels to stay warm, especially close to the kitchens of the buildings, where the garbage cans were outside for them to feed on. You would also see stray cats around the hospital grounds and they would help keep the rat problem in check.

Frank Jr. was getting bigger every day and Mom use to gather him up and go down to the Bronx to see her Mother and sometimes stay overnight. Giggy and Al would come up from Lenox Avenue to see Anna and the baby. Their Mother was not doing very well and it was a little over two years since Whitey died and she never got over losing her son. She loved Anna, but it wasn't the same. When Mom left home to get married and she wasn't there to fuss over, to talk to and just to be there. She was alone and Pop was no help either. He was getting older and slowing down, still drinking too much and could be a real pain in the ass most of the time, stubborn, belligerent and just plain nasty at times, a full blooded German who could not drink very well at all.

When Mom would come home from a visit with her Mother, Elsie would get very depressed and after a while she became very ill and passed away in the fall of 1937. She had made a pact with my Mother years before her death that she did not want to be buried on the same plot where Pop was going to be buried. They agreed that they would be buried together in the same grave when it was time for my Mother to pass on. Elsie was buried in a corner grave site of the Dawson plot and was interned into a double deep grave so that when it was Mom's time, she would be with her beloved Mother once more. Mom was lost for a long time; she had lost her best friend. Comforted by her cousins Alviena and Irma, she made it through her sorrow and she had Frankie and had her hands full with him and that took up a lot of time, not to think about her great loss. During this period, Mom became pregnant again and six weeks into the pregnancy she had a miscarriage, the fetus was a baby girl. She wanted a little girl that she could name Elsie and treat her as she was treated by her Mother, but this was not going to happen. She told herself that God had other plans for her baby girl and she trusted in God, believed in Him and would pray for her baby's soul. The doctors told Mom that she may not be able to have any more children and she said that she would leave that up to nature and the Lord.

Before they knew it, it was July of 1939 and on the 4th in Yankee Stadium, Lou Gehrig made his famous farewell speech when he said that he considered himself the luckiest man on the fact of the earth. He played first base for Columbia University and left college to play baseball for the New York Yankees. When he started with the team he was teased about his size, he was tall and lanky and Babe Ruth used to make fun of him until he started hitting the baseball as good if not better than Ruth. Lou was struck down with a cancer of the muscles and it was called Amyotrophic Lateral Sclerosis, which became known as Lou Gehrigs Disease, which he died from in 1941. Also in September 1939 on the first day Germany invaded Poland.

The world was going crazy and nobody knew when or where it was going to stop. A lot of nervous people in the government and on Wall Street were watching things going on in Europe. This could be very important for the economy in our country. One of the good things was the opening of Gone with the Wind at the movies in December, just before Christmas. This gave the country a change to take their minds off of Hitler and Europe.

Christmas was going to be a big one this year. Frankie was four years old and knew that Santa Claus was coming soon. He told his Mommy that he had been a good boy and that they should tell Santa to bring him everything he asked for in the letter that he and his Mommy had written and sent to the North Pole.

The winter that year was very cold, not a lot of snow, but frigid, and dad had to by extra coal for the furnace. January of 1940 started off fairly well, the roads were fairly bare, and dad would grab his son and head up to Spring Valley to see Grandma Dawson and George and Rob on Sunday mornings. Grandma's attitude had not changed much towards my mother. She softened up a little after Frankie was born but she still thought that mom wasn't the woman, she would have picked for her son. There was no love lost on my mother's side either, she knew what kind of woman Mary Dawson was, and was content to stay out of her way. Mom would stay home on those Sunday mornings and welcome the brake she had from her son. Her and grandma tolerated each other, and were civil to one another, for the sake of all concerned.

Dad had bought a newer car by then, a 1929 Hudson, R model, 4 door sedan, a real big car. Mom said you could get lost in the back seat, it was so big. They needed that size car, the way mom would pack up all the things needed for the baby. They didn't drive down to the city much to see pop or the boys. Now that Frankie was running, not walking anymore, it was hard to control him, and pop, Giggy or Al was not ready for that kind of mental abuse that a five year old could create.

Pop was alone now and getting along the best he could, with Elsie gone and went to work every day at the Waldorf.

CHAPTER 8

The town of Pearl River was growing by leaps and bounds with new streets being added and new buildings going up all over the little Hamlet. Quite a difference since Julius Braunsdorf, bought the large amount of land in 1870, which was then known as Muddy Brook. He had also started the Post Office in Pearl River NY. In 1872, after the famous pearls were found, and became the towns first Post Master. The town had a new school, rite in the middle of town on Central Avenue and on the end of the football field stood the Pearl River Hook and Ladder Fire house, which preceded the school, and was built in 1903. Sometime later in years, another fire house was built on the other side of town, over the train tracks, was the Excelsior Engine Company, organized in 1912.

1940 was a leap year, and I guess Germany thought that they should leap on Russia and invaded their country. Roberto Mussolini, from Italy, aligned himself with Adolf Hitler, agents Great Brittan and France in this part of World War Two. This invasion later on down the road would prove to be one of Hitler's biggest mistakes of the war.

Spring of 1941 was just around the corner and March was cold to start off with but towards the end of the month it became warmer. Mom was glad that the LORD made February; only twenty eight days long, because it was a very depressing month, cold and wet and Frank Jr. had to stay inside most of the time. March was getting warmer each day and mom was feeling strange, and had missed her time of the month and was getting concerned. She finally went to see the doctor. She couldn't be pregnant, the doctors told her after the miscarriage she had, years before, that she wouldn't be able to have any more children. Well the doctors were wrong, and the ways of the LORD, and nature prevailed, and mom was informed that she was going to have a baby some time in November.

How this could be, she thought, was this the chance to have the little girl she had miscarried, and wanted so badly. Her belief in GOD, told her it was real. She was nervous and scared all at the same time and didn't want to tell Dad; until she was sure everything would be ok with the baby. She waited a few more weeks and saw the doctor again during this time, just to make sure this was the miracle she had dreamt about years before. The doctor confirmed the good news once again and said that he saw no problem with her healthy condition.

Mom was starting to put on a little weight and thought that she should tell Dad the good news. She was a small woman and had lost most of the weight that she had put on while carrying Frankie, but it was five years later and she just wanted to make sure to watch her weight, stay as healthy as she could, and not take chances on another miscarriage. She told Dad, and at first he was upset about it, after the last pregnancy, and the doctors saying not to have any more kids. His attitude changed quickly when he heard what the doctor said about her health and that he thought that she would do just fine.

She had thought about going back to work before finding about the baby coming, but that was put on hold. Frankie had started kindergarten last year, and would be going into first grade when he turned six years old, the next September. That's when school started in Pearl River. The school was just two blocks away from Marten Place and Frankie would be able to walk there with a few other children that lived on the block. It wasn't back then, like it is today when you have to watch every move your kids make, and know where they are all the time. Perverts and child molesters were not that active in these years and things like that didn't happen. Frankie was happy when he was told that there was going to be possible a baby sister to play with in November. He told all his friends the good news, and couldn't wait until she arrived.

The spring went by quickly and seamed to go right into summer with hot weather. Mom had to carry the baby through the hot days and stay as cool as she could. Dad was busy at Rockland State Hospital, and when the new power house was completed, the state opened up some funding and started a maintenance department, for the facility. Carpenters shop, electrical shop and a plumbing shop along with a blacksmiths barn and forge. He saw his opportunity to get in on the ground floor, and switched over to work for the State of NY, in their plumbing shop. The money was a little less, but he would have full health insurance, a retirement plan and a secure working place for as long as he wanted. This meant a lot, with the new baby coming in the fall.

Shortly after he made the switch to work in the plumbing shop, he got deathly sick and he was taken off the job and taken directly to a hospital where he was diagnosed with Scarlet Fever. Well everybody got all excited. He would have to be quarantined in the hospital for at least two weeks, during that time he had lost all the hair on his body and it took the doctors four days to get his fever of 104* down to normal. They also worried about the new baby coming, and would this have any effect on it, or on mom. She was put into another hospital, to have tests taken and to make sure the baby would be ok. All her tests were ok and she went home after three days. Her doctor told her that there could be a problem with the baby, and we would have to wait and see. Mom did not like that news and became scared right off the bat. She was alone home with Frankie, with dad in quarantine and did not drive a car, she got in touch with Alviena, and they came and got her and young Frankie, to spend a few days at the farm in Bardonia. After she got there, she combed down, and her cousin made her feel at ease. Dad was released from the hospital after three weeks and had lost a lot of weight. He wasn't a real big man to begin with, 6ft.and about 180 lbs.

soaking wet. He was down to 155 when he got home and was very week. He had to stay home for another week to get some of his strength back, but after that he was getting ants in his pants, as they use to say, and had to get back to the job.

While he had been off that week, he and mom talked about the baby, about naming the baby Elizabeth Mary after the two Grandmothers and that was fine with him. They talked about how to make the one bedroom where Frankie was, roomier for the both of them for a while. But when the new born was brought home, a dresser draw would have to do for the time being. They still had Frank Jr's crib and they would fit it into his bedroom, with his small bed, when the time was right. Mom didn't pick out any boys names, and told dad that she knew it was a girl, she could tell the way it was kicking her inside. Mothers knew this these things and were always right. What the hell did he know, as long as the baby was healthy and had no effects from him having Scarlet Fever, it was ok with him.

Well the hot summer was coming to a close and September started with a little cooler weather. The family had a combined Labor Day, Frankie's Birthday party at the farm. Pop and the boys came up from the city and have a few beers. As usual a few beers got to be too many in the Runge family, and things almost got out of hand but mom got her Dutch up, and reminded them where they were and to behave themselves, or else. They did not fool with their baby sister when she got pissed off. Not even pop, and forget Dad, he was not about to get in the middle of this crap. All finally calmed down, and the party ended on a fairly good note.

Mom baked a cake for Frankie on his sixth birthday, and he was all set to start the first grade in school, the next day on September.11th in the year of 1941. He was getting to be a big boy and when he blew out the candles on his cake, he told his mommy that he had wished that his baby sister that was in her belly would come out soon so that he could play with her. Mom told him to pray to GOD, every night and in a few weeks or so GOD, will help mommy bring out the baby.

September was over and the weather started to change into fall with the changing of the leaves, all bright and different colors, red, yellow and brown. It was Mom's favorite time of year. Halloween was coming up and Frankie was planning to go out, trick or treating. He was going to be Hop a long Cassidy, the cowboy in the movies with his two six shooters. Mom got him all dressed up in his outfit, guns and all. Then out they went, up and down the block with his brown paper bag for candy treats following the other Moms and Dads, going door to door with little ghosts, tramps, princesses and all sorts of costumes. She got tired real quick, the baby within her was getting huge and her little legs wore out easily. It was almost dusk when they got back to the house. They separated the candy from the pennies he had gotten and Mommy put them into his piggy bank, about a dollar and sixty cents. He was rich, that's what he told Daddy when he got home from work.

November was here and Mom was getting close to having her little girl. She went to the doctors office for a checkup and all was well, he told her that he thought that the baby wouldn't be here until the first week of December, to go home and rest as much as possible.

Mom told Dad what Dr. Leftcawitz said about resting and December and that everything looked fine. They started to plan for Thanksgiving dinner and were thinking about have Pop and the boys up from New York City. Dad was going to Spring Valley early that day to see his Mother and to see if brother George would like to come over for turkey that afternoon. Grandma Dawson wouldn't come over, she had to take care of Robert and had no interest in seeing her daughter in law anyway. That was ok with Mom, no big loss. George said that he would be there that day and looked forward to it.

President Franklin d Roosevelt declared this Thanksgiving Day and November 26th, 1941 the first official Thanksgiving holiday in the United States. Dad went and got a nice big turkey and was going to have it cooked at the bakery down town so Mom didn't have to cook it and that was fine with her. She would make the stuffing and the vegetables and that was okay with her too. Well, the best laid plans of mice and men do go astray. The turkey did not get cooked, at least not on the 26th and not at the bakery, because surprise, surprise on Saturday night at 9 o'clock, Mom had to go to the hospital with labor pains. Dad was nervous as hell and had to wait down stairs in the waiting room. He was there about three hours, smoking one cigarette after another until just after midnight on November 22. At 12:07am the baby was born and Mom was fine and the baby was fine also.

All was real fine except for one small fact. When the doctor came down to tell Dad the good news, he informed him that he was the proud father of a big bouncing baby boy. That's right Boy! Mom was just waking up and still drowsy, she knew about the baby and the name was not going to be Elsie after her Mother. To say that she was happy that all was well with the baby and that there were no side effects from the Scarlet Fever that Dad had. That's how I came into the world with the help of God, Mom and the good doctor.

Now what to name the big surprise. They only picked out girls names, because Mom just knew it was going to be a girl, she could tell, the way it kicked inside of her. Mom wasn't wrong too often, but she missed the boat on this one. Well, it was Alvin William Dawson, me named after Uncle George Alvin Dawson and Pop William Runge. Thank god it was not Elsie. We stayed in the hospital for three days and then it was home to Martin Place and of course the large dresser drawers in Mom and Dads room. Frankie was staying with a close friend while I was born and when he found out that I wasn't a girl, he told Mommy to send me back to God, because God had made a mistake and sent the wrong baby. Mommy explained to him that God does not make mistakes and that Mommy was wrong, she thought it was a baby girl in her belly, but it was really a beautiful baby boy instead. He finally said that it was okay with him to have a little brother to play with and couldn't keep his eyes off the baby.

Five days after we got home from the hospital, mom and I went to the doctor's office for a follow up visit for her and me. The doctor said that I was just fine, but because mom had such a hard delivery, he had to do some extra surgery and sewing that he told her that she would not have any more children. Well she had heard that story once before and I came along. He assured her that this time, it was a fact.

She was a little depressed that she wouldn't be able to have her little girl, to fuss over, but it was ok because THE LORD gave her a healthy baby boy instead, and she believed in her GOD, and HE answered her prayers and her baby was healthy. All was right at home, mom, dad, and Frankie were happy with the new baby, but all wasn't right in the world and two weeks after I was born, on SUNDAY.DECEMBER.7TH 1941, just a little after 7am, Hawaii Time, THE IMPERIAL EMPIRE OF JAPAN attacked and boomed PEARL HARBOR. The Japanese used 353 planes in the attack in which they sunk four battle ships, many others damaged, and many air craft destroyed. About twenty four hundred people were killed in the attack. The next day, PRESIDENT ROOSERVELT declared war on Germany and Japan and I was only two week old. I don't know if this was a bad omen or not. The country was just getting over the depression years and now we were going into war. We could not let Hitler or Japan get away with this horrific act, and kill twenty four hundred innocent people.

All the people in the UNITED STATES were mad about PEARL HARBOR and war being declared. Young men were joining the armed forces right and left to go fight for their country. A lot of people of Japanese descent were gathered up and sent to internment camps all over the country to make sure that there were no spy's among us. Many of these folks were good AMERICANS, and some were not. A lot of German people also were looked at carefully, and some were found to be spies. My Grandfather Runge, being a German immigrant also feared for his safety, but he was older now, had a good job and was well known and liked by important people.

It was good that he had these connections and he loved his country, the UNITED STATES, and was said that the people in the old country were following this tyrant Hitler and this other war monger Mussolini into a war they could not win. Dad and Uncle George were probably get drafted into the service, and they got sent their notice to report to the draft board and went down. Uncle George couldn't go because he was the sole support of his mother and brother Rob and they didn't want Dad because he had Scarlet Fever and he was classified 4F and both were sent home. The war progressed and by the time I was two years old, Dad had gotten a second job, back at Lederle Labs, part time, helping to make medicine for the wounded soldiers at war. He also joined the CIVIL DEFENCE GROUP, to help direct folks to shelters in case we were attacked by bombers or any other emergency.

I was coming up on three years old now and it was getting quite cramped in the small bedroom with my big brother Frankie. He was almost nine years old and all my toys were taking up his space, as he put it to mommy. My crib had been converted into some kind of small bed, Dad was handy at adapting things, like cribs, and a lot of other things, and anyway it was too crowded in the room. Mom had made up her mind; it was time to get a bigger house. Of course she didn't say anything to Dad, she would tell him when she had found a house that she wanted and the she would let him know, in her normal, gentle way that we were moving. This is the way that she knew how to get around arguing with my father and it worked.

They were both busy by this time; Mommy had gotten her job back at Lederle, part time during the day, about four hours. She had found a nice next door neighbor to watch me at these hours and if she was late for any reason, it was ok with the woman. Frankie was in school all day by then, in the fourth grade, and she would be home by the time school got out for the day.

CHAPTER 10

Well in moms spare time , she went house hunting with one of her friends from town, Gertrude, and they spent about two weeks looking before they found a nice three bedroom house at 50 Ridge Street. It was a two story house, three bedrooms up stairs, kitchen, living room and dining room down stairs. It was just what the doctor ordered. Now all she had to do was to tell Frank Sr. That we were going to move. Easier said, and then done. The rent was a little more than at Martin Place, but the house was almost twice the size, and as far as mom was concerned, it was a done deal. She gave the owner a deposit on the next month's rent and then she will tell dad tonight, while he is relaxed and sitting in his easy chair.

Dad was sitting down, a good thing too, when mommy broke the news about the house on Ridge Street. Well he moaned and groaned about it for a few minutes, but after a while when he got calmed down, he realized that Martin Place was getting to small for the family and since they didn't own this house, he wasn't going to put any money into it. He and mommy and of course us two boys drove down to see our new home. He did not know that mom put a deposit on the house yet, but that's the way mom did things. He liked the house. It was big and it had a garage, he liked that very much. He could store his tools in there, and a place to work on things or just to get out of the house for a while to himself.

The rent was higher than he thought it would be, or should be, but you have to understand that dad was cheap, well frugal is a better word. After thinking it over a short time, he told mom to get a hold of the owner and give them a deposit on it and they would move in the first of the next month. She said that she would do just that and told him to give her twenty five dollars, for the deposit. She already gave the owner fifteen, and put the other ten dollars in the cookie jar for a rainy day. Mommy was great, she knew just how to get around dad and it saved a lot of arguing, most of the time. The following month we moved down to our new home and started to make friends with the neighbors and get use to the new location only a block from town.

Ridge Street was a quiet street just off of Franklin Ave. It ran north and south, parallel to Main Street and it was about three quarters of a mile long, south down to Gilbert Ave. William Street was behind our house ,and also ran north and south, down to Gilbert. This is the way that Mr. Braunsdorf set up many of the streets of MUDDY BROOK before it became PEARL RIVER. The houses were pretty much the same design, some bigger, but a lot of look a likes down the whole street. Many of these houses were built to house employees of Brounsdorf's factory, Dexter Folder Co. just two blocks away. Back then, in the early forties the roads were not black topped, but were oiled with heavy black oil and then gravel was spread on top to make a kind of smooth surface. The gravel would collect on the side of the road and everybody went out and scooped it up and put in their driveways.

Frankie liked the new house; he had his own bedroom as did I. I had the smaller one, but that was ok because it was close to mommy and daddy's room and since I was still a little afraid of the dark it was great. Mommy always left a night light on for me. She always made sure that I was safe and that she was close by if I needed her. The bathroom was close to my room too, and that worked out just fine in case I had an emergency during the night. I really liked the new home and I knew that mom liked it too. It was easy to walk to the store for milk and bread and all the people were very friendly. It was nice.

A lot of people on Ridge Street already knew each other, two boys next door were going to school with Frankie and a girl across the street was in the same class, her name was Rita and her Mother and Father worked at Rockland State Hospital, where Dad worked. Mom's good friend Gertrude lived four blocks away on Main Street. Her husband worked at Dexter's factory and they had four sons. One son was in my brother's class and one of the other sons was my age. She had her hands full with her boys as Mom did with her two sons.

It was a shorter walk to school for Frankie than it was on Martins Place, all he had to do was walk through our back yard, go across William Street and get on the path through a small wooded area and go across Franklin Avenue right by the school about a five minute walk. Mom said that he was growing like a weed. He was going to be tall like his Uncle bill, who was 6'2". He was very active at school, always playing baseball at the school field with other ten year old boys and missed dinner most of the time because he couldn't hear his mother calling him that it was ready. He would catch hell all the time and ate a lot of cold dinners. He didn't seem to mind much, he loved baseball. They would even play stickball on Ridge Street, in front of the house and have to make sure that they didn't get hit by a car. Made Mommy nervous as hell, but they were going to play anyway. I was almost five years old and was getting ready for school.

On May 8th.1945, Germany surrendered to the combined forces in World War II. Hitler had committed suicide in Berlin, to evade being captured. Mussolini was caught in Italy, dressed as a woman and was hiding in the back of a truck. He was tried, and put to death, by hanging by his own countrymen. Japan still fought on in the war and refused to give in. The summer was a very warm one and the July 4th celebrations in the country were many, but marred by the fact that we were still fighting the Japanese in the Pacific, many of our troops were dying and that had to stop.

August had arrived and The President, Harry Truman, had made a major decision. On the 6th of August, he ordered that the Atom Bomb, be dropped the Japanese city of Hiroshima, and on August .8th, another bomb, be dropped on the city of Nagasaki. Millions of people were killed and Japan was devastated. By this act of war, Truman saved many of our solders lives. On August 15th, 1945, Japan surrendered and the war was finally over. In Europe during the war, Hitler had exterminated over six million Jews and tried to erase them from the face of the earth. Thank GOD he failed, but in doing this he committed the worst crime on humanity the world has ever seen. Our boys were coming home. It was September, I was two months short of five years old, but I could start school, and was going into Kindergarten. I was really getting excited and could hardly wait.

My teacher was Miss Jersey and I thought that she was great. She looked a lot like Mommy and she like me too. I had a few friends that lived on Ridge and William Streets and we all would walk to school together the same way Frankie did. We all went to the same school on Central Avenue.

Dad was settled in a pretty good in his garage with his plumbing tools and he had bought a 1939 Chevy pickup truck so that he could carry his tools to the side jobs we has doing to make extra money. Remember, I told you Dad was not lazy and would make a buck whenever he could. He did a lot of work for Mr. Ablondi across the street. He had a tavern on Main Street called Ablondi's Bar and the back door to the tavern let out onto Ridge Street. He also owned five small stores in the same row as the bar, with a small house that he rented at the end of the stores. Dad did a lot of plumbing jobs for him and his stores, and became good friends with the Ablondi family. Their home was also on Ridge Street about two blocks from ours. Right next to our house and Mr. and Mrs. Spooner, a very nice Italian family. They all called John Spooner, sponajohn, he spoke broken English and was very friendly to all of us. He had a very big garden, all kinds of vegetables and he took pride in it and would work in it most of the day. He was retired and all he did was to take care of the garden and the big six bedroom house, next to ours. Between the two houses there were two big cherry trees and would bring forth gobs of cherries for both families, for pies, jams and jellies. Mom could bake a great cherry pie and would jar up lots of jam for us and her friends.

We had a big back yard and Dad decided to build a chicken coop and raise chickens for their eggs and to eat them. He started out small, one rooster and about six hens. That was the first two weeks. Then he got dangerous, and bought another rooster and a dozen more hens. Now he was on a roll. It really took off and we had an abundance of eggs, which he ended up trading with Spooner John for veggies. This worked out great. The war was over, money was tight, and everybody had gardens, chickens, or ducks and some even would raise hogs, to trade off for other things. Some of the smaller farms would have cows, for milk and cream and even beef stock for meat.

Dad had this thing; he would not feed anything that didn't feed him back. If a hen didn't lay any eggs for three days in a row, he would put a rubber band around that hen's neck and on Sundays when he was off work, he would slaughter them. We always had chicken to eat and to swap with Mr. Spooner. He would take me out to the coop and show me how to gather the eggs, and I was always to bring rubber bands with me. Frankie did this once in a while, but the coop stunk too much and the smell made him sick. Yup, he was a smart boy!! I use to do the egg thing, before I went to school and sometimes after. I liked to feed them and it was fun to watch them scurry around for the feed. This was a good time in my life, as I recall. Daddy always worked hard and mommy did too, and she gave us boys all the love in the world and kept us safe all the time.

CHAPTER 11

Pop was getting on in years now, and him, Uncle Giggy and Al came up to Pearl River very seldom. Pop had moved into a small, cheep hotel, near the boys on Lenox Ave, after Elsie, passed away. His health was failing and he had to only work part time. He was seventy years old, but had a lot of hard miles on him, with smoking and drinking too much, all those years. It was time for him to stop work. Mom and dad had talked it over and went to Spooner- John to see if pop could rent a room in his big house. Mr. Spooner had converted the upstairs of his house into small one bedroom flats. Dad had done some plumbing for him and the one flat would be just great for pop. The stairs were the only problem, but pops legs were still ok, and he could get up and down them fine.

Mom told Giggy what was going to happen, and pop was fine with the whole thing. The day of the big move, Giggy got one of his old cronies from the bar he worked in, and loaded pop's belongings into this guy's old truck and with pop, the three of them came to Ridge Street. Uncle Al stayed in the city, with his bad hip, all he would do is get in the way. So pop became our new neighbor and things were working out fine until he started telling mom how to run her home and bring up her kids.

Well Pop should have kept his thoughts to himself and mom went off on him so bad. She thought she might as well do it right the first time, and get it over with. She reminded him that he was far from the father of the year when her and her brothers were growing up, and that she was a woman now, not a little girl, to be taken care of, and that bringing up her two sons was her business, and not his, because he didn't do such a great job with his own sons. That was that, pop never got the German up in mom's temper again.

Dad would still take Frankie and me for a ride to see Grandma Dawson and Uncle George and Rob on Sunday mornings. Grandma was ill and Rob was failing also. George told both his brothers that he was concerned about their mother, and in late December of 1945 she passed away and was buried next to her husband John, in the family plot at New Hempstead. My father took his mother's passing very hard, and that there was no love lost between her and my mother, mommy tried to console dad the best she could. Mom was not a vises person, but if you rubbed her the wrong way once, you didn't get another shot at her. She saw to that. I was over five years old when she died and then Uncle George took over the care of Robert, which was hard on him, with his work and all. George never married, and now more than ever, looked forward to our Sunday visits. Looking back, I think he was a real lonely person. He loved Frankie and me very much, though he never said so.

Uncle Rob was a nice man, quiet and stayed much to himself. He liked seeing Dad and us when we visited, and I'm sure he loved Frankie and me also. He liked that I was named after George's middle name Alvin ,and I think he liked me the best because I would sit by him for a while when we were there. After a year or so, after his mother's death, he became very sick and had to go to the hospital, where he lingered a long time, and he died in early 1947. He also was buried at the family plot, next to his mother and father. This left George all alone at the homestead, in Spring Valley, where the whole Dawson family grew up. It was a said time.

Giggy and Al would come up from the city to see Poppy and mom and spend the day on Saturdays or a Sunday. Mommy would cook dinner, chicken of course and mom would tell me to go over to Mr. Ablondi's back door, and knock on it, and wait for him to open it. She would send with me, two small tin pales, called GROWLERS, which would hold beer in them, with lids on top, so that it would not spill out. This I did often when my uncles came from the city. My mother and her brothers, all loved beer and poppy was no stranger to it either. I did what I was told, grabbed the pales and knocked on the back door of the tavern. Mr. Ablondi came to the door, told me to stay there, and he returned in a short while with two full growlers of beer. I gave him the thirty cents that Giggy gave me, to pay for both pales. When I got back home, he gave me a dime for going. I was rich!!

Dad didn't drink that much because he couldn't drink well at all. Two or three glasses were his limit. He would get shit faced rather quick, and the fall asleep. That was fine with mom; she had seen enough drinking and drunks in her life, and not to be married to one, suited her just fine. Her brothers and her father were drinkers, and nasty ones at that. She was the best drinker in the whole Runge tribe, and they all knew it. Mom loved beer, could drink a lot and could hold it very well for a small person. After I was born, mommy didn't lose a lot of weight, she wasn't fat, just well rounded, and only being five foot tall, looked heavier then she really was. Unlike the rest of the Runge's, she didn't get nasty, just mellow.

They were drinking pretty heavy this time. I had to make four more trips across the street to Ablondi's back door. The clincher was when pop brought out a bottle of schnapps and the men drank that, with the beer. Dad was sleeping in the living room chair by then, and things started to get testy at the dining room table. Mom saw what was coming, and she put a stop to the crap, before it got started. She reminded them all, that this was her home, and they could go into the living room, and sleep it off, and go home, to the city in the morning. Pop got his German up, and decided to go to his rooms next door, at the Spooners. He was just shit faced enough to be a real pain in the ass for my mother. I watched him cross the yard, and he made it to the front door ok.

The two brothers did what they were told and went to the living room to sleep it off, with dad. They knew better then to mess with their baby sister. She had put them in their places before, and believe me they did not want a refresher course. They left early the next morning; dad did the egg run and went to work. Frankie went down to the cellar to get the two pales of old ashes from the furnace, to spread in the drive way. That was one of his jobs. The pals were too heavy for me to tote up the stairs. I would go down with daddy sometimes to watch him stoke the furnace, knowing that someday I would be doing that job, and bring up the ashes.

I would sit for hours in the kitchen, watching mommy cook. She was a very good cook, and told me to watch her closely, because someday I may have to cook for myself. I learned a lot from all those hours in the kitchen. I sure knew how to cook chicken, and a lot of ways too. We were pals, her and I. She us to call me [her bestes-pal]. That made me feel special. I loved her so much. She always cooked enough food for us and she would make up a plate for poppy next door. I would run it over to him before we sat to the table. Sometimes he wasn't home and I would have to go over and knock on Mr. Ablondi's back door and have them tell pop that dinner was delivered and to get it while it was still hot. Poppy did have a tendency to go across the street and linger at the tavern to long, and forget to go home. Sometimes he would meet my daddy there for a beer or two.

Like I said before, Dad was not a drinker and three was his limit. Poppy on the other hand thought he had no limit. A lot of times, Dad would have to go across the street and usher pop up to the room. Big brother Frank Jr. sometimes had to do this duty also. This did not please my mother, but as long as he didn't get hurt, she tolerated it. Mr. Ablondi knew when to cut pop off, and watched over him. They were both immigrants, and understood the ways of growing their families up in their new country, America.

Poppy would get on this good behavior kick and not go across the street to much. He told me to go around the neighborhood and collect all the brown bottles I could find and bring them to him. I got about a dozen, and he gave me a nickel for each one. He asked Dad to pick up a bushel of green and ripe apples when he went up to Spring Valley. Back then all the spare land were apple orchards, and Conklin's Orchard was the biggest around. Dad did as pop had asked, got the apples and asked mommy what the hell pop was doing with all those apples. The following week, the same thing, more bottles and more apples, finally, mom had enough and had to find out what the hell was going on with pop. Well ,come to find out pop had a still going on in the kitchen sink, in his flat, and was making apple jack booze. Well mom flipped out, he was selling the stuff to some of his old crony friends, on the two blocks and even some customers from up in town. The Pearl River Hotel Bar customers got wind of the business pop had going on, and they were coming down to buy some hooch.

It got so bad, with poppy making the apple jack, that the one liquor store owners told dad that pop had to stop making the stuff, it was hurting his business. Pop stopped and things quieted down. My brown bottle collecting came to a halt.

Shortly after that time, poppy became very ill. The doctor told him and mom, that he had to stop drinking and smoking that GOD awful LIBERTY, pipe tobacco. It was killing him, and it finally did do just that. When he passed away, we went up to the flat to clean it out and found fifteen brown bottles of apple jack, curing in a dark closet. He started out brewing beer in Germany and ended up making booze here in the U S. I missed him, he was my buddy.

CHAPTER 12

I was about nine years old when poppy died. Frankie was fifteen and was wrapped up with sports all over the place. Dad had built him a basketball back board and net on a pole, in the back yard. They got some garden lime and marked out the boarders and the foul line. It looked pretty sharp. The next door neighbor's boys, Jim and Pat, would come over with some other kids and they would choose up teams and play well into the evening. Mom would have trouble getting him in for dinner, and then blame dad for building the dam thing. She didn't really mind, but it sounded good. There could have been a lot of other things he could have been doing a lot worse than playing ball in the back yard and the neighbors family's felt the same way.

He was good at basketball and baseball too. He even got his picture in the LEDERLE magazine one month, swinging a bat while in a makeup game out on their field. Mom and dad were proud of that, because they both had worked at the plant during the war. One of his home town hero's was Bruno Ablondi, who lived just down the street from us.

Bruno was one of two sons that Mr. Ablondi had. His one son Mario went to Pear River High School a few years ahead of Bruno who graduated in 1947. He was a gifted, athlete and was ALL COUNTY, in football, basketball and baseball. I remember him slightly, but Frankie idolized him, and wanted to be just like him.

The Korean War started in June of 1950, and ended in July of 1953. Almost thirty seven thousand of our troops were killed. One of them was Bruno, and the whole town went into shock, he was loved by all. Frankie was devastated, his hero was gone forever. I think that's what drove him to be a good athlete himself. The family closed the tavern for a week, while the mourned their son. Mario, the oldest son, stayed on to work for his father at the bar, for many years, until his dad passed away. They were a nice family.

Frankie was in high school in 1951, his second year and playing junior varsity sports, and doing very well. His coach Ira Shuttelworth liked him and knew that he was going on to bigger and better things as a junior and senior. He was the center on the football team, guard on the basketball team and catcher on the baseball team. Three sports, like his hero Bruno. In the spring of 1952, I was ten years old and was playing a lot of baseball myself, with a lot of my buddies. One of my friends found out that we could play baseball for his uncle, Harry Jackson, in a junior league at the Memorial Park in Spring Valley. We had about nine players and were ready to go and play.

1952 and we all were about ten and eleven years old. We had a chance to play ball together as a team for the first time, ever, and we even won the league championship that year. It was chance to play ball together as a team for the first time, ever, and we even won the league championship that year. Mr. Jackson even got us uniforms, we were hot stuff. Whenever we had a game, we would all ride our bikes to Jay's house, and his mother would pile us all in her old Studebaker car, and off we'd go to Spring Valley. Jay was our third baseman. There was Chucky, Teddy, Frankie, Larry, Johnny and me as well as Jacky and Gene Jackson, Harry's two sons. After the season was over we had a party at restaurant that we would never forget.

The following year a fellow named Art Hopper, and some business men started the Pearl River Little League in our town. They built a baseball field down by the original Muddy Brook. The land donated by the Dexter Company. We had dug-outs, bleachers and a fence around the whole field. It was sharp. Only one thing wrong, all us boys that played together in Spring Valley, had to split up and play for different teams of the league. Frankie, Jay and Sammy, went to other teams, but Chuck, Larry and I stayed together, and played for the same team. Chuck and I were in the homerun race that year, and I beat him out with eleven homers, he only had eight. Teddy and Johnny couldn't play that year because they were too old. You had to be born before a certain date to be eligible to play that year. That was a shame, we all missed them. My team, the Giants, only finished in second place.

While I was playing little league baseball that summer, my big brother Frank was playing American Legion Baseball in Rockland County. He was playing first base and catching on and off. He was getting to become a very good player and in his up and coming senior year, Coach Shuttelworth or Uncle Ira as everybody called him, expected Frankie to be selected for All County Baseball and he was. That was the spring of 1953. Football and big brother excelled at that too, and in a game agents Nyack High School he punted a 79 yard kick, the longest to this day in Rockland County. Uncle Ira coached all three sports back then and had brother playing basketball too. This was his favorite sport, played all four in his high school year. He loved the game, had a good outside set shot and could rebound with the best of players. I guess Dad building that basketball makeshift court and backboard in the back yard did pay off. We all went to his games when we could, Dad had to work a lot of those times, but Mommy and I went.

He did not equal his hero's records, but Bruno would have been proud of him, I know that my family was. During his high school years he found another hero, Uncle Ira. He looked up to him and wanted to be a coach just like him. After graduating high school in 1953, he could have had a shot to go to Michigan State, but because of financial funds, he could only afford to go to a state college in upstate New York. Cortland State was a good school and had a great basketball team. That was right up his alley. He excelled there also.

The town was changing back then. Ridge Street was now paved with black top as well as most of the other streets. New businesses were coming into town and new buildings being built. A far cry from the time that Mr. Braunsdoff had first bought the parcel of swamp land in 1870 and started to lay out the roads and build his sewing machine factory in the middle of town. At that time the majority of people that came to the new town were of German and Scandinavian decent, machinists and skilled workers that came to work in his factory, to build his machines. But this would change, more and more folks would work at Lederle. The town was on the move in the upward direction. With the increase in population came new zoning laws. One new law said that Dad's chicken coop had to go, as well as all the others, at private houses. Gardens were ok, but not chickens. After all the years of putting ashes from the furnace on the ground of the pen, around the coop, Dad decided to plant a small garden. With all that chicken shit that was spread out over the years, and the ashes, it was a prime spot. He turned over the mixture and dirt, and put in three dozen tomato plants and some corn seeds. Needless to say that he didn't need any fertilizer for his garden. Spooner john gave him some pointers on gardening, and with all that fertile ground Dad had tomatoes the size of softballs, and corn for us the whole year. He would do the same as he would with the chickens, trade off for other veggies and fruit. Our time, growing up on Ridge Street, was the nicest part of my life and the memories I have, will last forever.

CHAPTER 13

The summer that Frankie graduated from school, he and some of his friends started a softball team and entered the team into the Pearl River Softball League; the team was The Campus, which was a soda shop across from the high school on Central Avenue. All the students hung out there and Bill King, the owner was glad to sponsor the boys to play ball. They played in the evenings, right on the field in front of the high school. The teams were made up of local merchants that sponsored them and also played. It started to draw some pretty good crowds to watch the games on the summer nights. The league was small, only four teams to start with, but the games became very competitive and as time passed, other teams outside Pearl River wanted to join the league. The county was growing rapidly now, because of two things, one thing was the bridge over the Hudson River.

The Tappan Zee BRIDGE crossed the HUDSON RIVER at Nyack NY. , and ended at Tarrytown, NY. Separating Rockland from Westchester County The crossing was part of the NEW YORK STATE THRUWAY road system and made it an easy commute from Orange and Rockland Counties, into New York City. After the bridge was completed in 1955, many people moved to our town and others in Rockland, to get out of the city. The environment was better for the children, the schools were safer and the housing was reasonable. A lot of these people were city cops and fireman; they had good jobs and could afford to bring their families up in the safe suburbs. They would commute by car, local buses or even trains to their jobs.

Shortly after the Tappan Zee Bridge opened for traffic, the PALASADES INTERSTATE PARKWAY opened in August of 1958. This was another major route to the city and ran from the Orange County line into NEW JERSEY, to the GEORGE WASHINGTON BRIDGE. This was also an easy commute. A lot of these police officers that moved to our town from the city, played softball there, and wanted to have a team in our league. Well the league grew and we went from playing, not only evening games, but started to play on Sunday mornings also. We had to use more school fields to do this, and the Town of Otangetown Recreation Department, and the school system, said ok to our plans and we were using four different fields every Sunday. The new police team was called Reese Beer Sales, and they were good and became heavy rivals with the young Campus team.

The young Campus team started to get a few young players fresh out of other high schools and even some, still in school, and started playing softball in other leagues throughout Rockland County. They would enter fast pitch and slow pitch leagues, where ever they could. Frank was getting a reputation as a very good fast pitch, or windmill pitcher as it was called, and other teams sought him out to play for their team. He was tall, with a blond, flat top crew cut and they all called him by his nick-name DIXIE, which he picked up in high school. He commanded a large presents from the pitchers rubber, standing at 6"foot 6 inches tall and weighing about two hundred pounds. This playing softball, and working for a roofer at Rockland State Hospital took up most of his time, in the summer, before he was to leave for college.

He left for Cortland State, in late August to sign in for the football team, his freshman year. Dad had gotten him a 1941 Oldsmobile, during the summer and made sure that it was in good enough shape to make the two hundred mile trips back and forth to Cortland. Dad still was working two jobs, to help offset the college expenses. He didn't make the varsity team the first year, but he did the second. He could still punt the ball, and would do that throughout the four years in college. After football, came basketball season, his first love. They had a very good varsity team; he made the squad but was not a starter on the team that year.

After the first year away at school, Frank came home to work on the roofs again. This kept him in shape to play more softball, and also play basketball in a summer league at BEAR MOUNTAIN STATE PARK. There were about ten teams entered, they would play at night, outside, and the court was all lit up with big lights. They had some big crowds come to watch the teams play. They came from all over the state and some from NY City. Dixie's team was good, all from Rockland County, men that he had played agents in high school. They were not quite good enough. They met their match agent's two teams from the city, all black players, and could they play the game. They would run and run, up and down the court, and shoot the ball and before the ball cleared the net, they would be on their way back down the court. They were really good and brother said that he learned a lot about the game from those teams. He had a pretty full summer that year. He would take me with him to Bear Mountain some nights, to watch the games. They sometimes had three games in a night and if he played the early game, I could go, that way I'd be home early, because I was only thirteen and mom wanted me home before eleven at night. I looked up to my big brother, and loved him very much. He never hurt me or abused me in any way, and I tried to understand why I couldn't hang around with him more often. I was just too young.

I often think how it would have been, if were only a year apart in age, and if we played on the same teams together, how it would have turned out. I was not the athlete that he was.

71

We were still on Ridge Street and mommy would take me with her down to the city to see Uncle Giggy and Al. they were not doing too well. All those hard years were taking its toll on both of them. Al was sickly, very thin and very pale. He went to the VA hospital and they told him that he drank too much, and he smoked too much, and he had an inflamed liver. Giggy told him that he could have told him all those things, without going to the VA. Those two could be like oil and water at times and other times, like cream and coffee, but not when they are drinking. We'd stay a few hours and then catch the subway uptown, and then take the bus back to Pearl River.

Frank was in his second year at college. Dad and I would drive up to the cemetery and visit the graves of the family and then we would come back to the homestead to see Uncle George. He would give me money to vacuum the house for him, and dust off the furniture too. He use to have Frankie do it, but I was to do it now that he was away. That was great with me; I had no problem making five bucks. He was going to make the house into a two family.

An apartment upstairs, and wanted Dad to run the plumbing for the new kitchen upstairs.

Dad did this and remodeled the bathroom, downstairs while they were at it. The work came out fine; I even helped, a little! The apartment was rented to a newly married couple. She was a real good looking gal. They rented there two years and then bought a house. By this time George was not well, Authorities had filled his body, his hands, knees and back.

He was about ready to retire. He did small jobs, made some cabinets at home and would do most of the work in his garage. Dad told mommy that he was worried about him and he would get up to see him more frequently.

CHAPTER 14

The mid 50's were not very good years for the Dawson family at all. They say bad things come in three's, well it did for us. First, Giggy called from the city to tell mom that Al was dead, and could she come down. Apparently they were across the street, in their local hang out bar, drinking of course, they got into an argument and Al got pissed off and left. By then, according to Giggy, he was shit-faced, went across the street to their hotel, which was a one room flop house, to his room on the second floor. He went in and said something derogatory to the hotel clerk, and started up the stairs. Well he got to the first landing, lost his balance and fell backwards down the stairs to the bottom, and broke his neck. It being an accident, the police had to take the body to the Bell View Hospital Morgue, and it had to be identified by a family member. Well Giggy was too drunk to do it, so he called his baby sister. Mommy always was the one called, when poppy, or any of the boys got in trouble. She took over for her mom, after Elsie died. Mom was the rock that would not break, for both families. They informed mom that they would have to perform an autopsy on Al, because of the way he died.

Mom informed the Veterans Authority that Al had died and where the body was taken. They told her that they would take care of burring him as soon as they were allowed to get the body from Bell View. This took a week and then the funeral was set, and he was buried by his father and brother Whitey, at New Hempstead. The doctor that performed the autopsy told mom that Al's liver was 98% gone from the drinking and his hip was so deteriorated, that it was a wonder that he could walk at all ,and that he must have been in a lot of pain. After the funeral, Giggy went back to the city and continued his same old life style.

Shortly after that, Uncle George became very ill and suddenly passed away at the homestead in Spring Valley. Dad was beside himself and took his death very hard. George, having no one else in his life, left everything to his younger brother, Frank. Dad set up the funeral, and George was buried next to his mother in the family plot. Dad decided to rent out both apartments in the house, and become a land lord. This worked for a while, but was not trouble free, as he soon found out.

Spring Valley was mostly a Jewish town and they owned a lot of houses, and rented the too mostly minority folks. This made it hard for my father to rent out the apartments. Nobody back then, wanted to live in a minority neighborhood. Dad was not good at being a landlord either, he was too soft, compared to George, who would set down certain rules, and if you didn't abide by them, you'd be gone.

This was not working out to well for dad. His renters were beating the shit out of the homestead, and running behind in the rent. He had to make a move pretty soon, while the house was still standing.

About this time, bad news number three came along in the form of Giggy. His one lung had collapse and was taken to the hospital. He almost died. He had holes in his lungs, and had to be put on a breathing machine to live. Once again mommy got the call and rushed to the city, with me in tow. I was only coming up on my fourteenth birthday, and she was not leaving me at home alone. She left Dad a note and we were gone. She talked to the doctor down there and he said that he would have to go into a special lung hospital. The only one we had close by was Summit Park Hospital, in Pomona. N Y. Mom got lucky, or Giggy did, they had room for him, and they transported him from the city, to Pomona. They put him on a breathing machine, and he stayed on it for a long time. Smoking five packs of Pall Mall cigarettes a day, finally took its toll. Dad went down to the hotel, where his room was with mom, to pick up his things, which wasn't that much and stored it in the garage at Ridge Street. He was inhaling medication and could stay off of the machine a few hours a day, until the med's worn off and then it was back on the breather. This went one for about six months and his body started to break down, till finally the end was near. The doctor called mom to let her know the bad news.

Mom knew the news was coming, but not that soon. After just burring Al, and then George, and now Giggy was failing. It didn't look very good. Mom and I talked about it and I asked her about Robert, Giggy's son, from his marriage years ago. We decided to get in touch with Robert, and inform him that his father was dying and where he was. His mother and father's marriage, and divorce ended with a lot of hostility on both sides. But this was the time to see him, if he wanted too, to say good bye. We left it up to him. He called mom a few days after he'd seen his father and was grateful to us for telling him about Giggy's bad health. Mom and I went to see him the next day at the hospital, he was smiling and told mom that his Bobby came to see him and that he stayed all afternoon, they talked and cried together ,and it was wonderful. Before we left and said goodbye, I turned to look at him and noticed that he had a glow on his face. It was the strangest thing I had ever seen. I told mom about it and she noticed it too. That night, Giggy passed away in his sleep. Mommy was at peace with his death, and we buried him with poppy and his two brothers. Many years later, Frankie and I had some bronze plates made up, with dates of births, and deaths and I made up concrete forms to set the plates on. This way they wouldn't be buried in unmarked graves. I visit them when I can also. Three hard parts of our lives, almost back to back, in a short time. But it wasn't over.

It is said that bad news travels in threes. This wasn't true in our case. When the Tee Zee Bridge opened, and also the two parkways , heading south ,to get to the city, it not only made it an easy commute but it meant a lot more impact on Rockland County residents. Property and school taxes went up dramatically; all the rents for housing rose, and property and home prices went out of sight. We were renting the house on Ridge Street, and the owner wanted to sell it to dad, at a price that dad could not afford. The owner saw an opportunity to make a killing on the house, and he did.

We didn't have much choice, dad had the homestead in Spring Valley, which he owned out right, which George left him, with income from the apartment up stairs and Frankie still in college, we had to cut corners and move to the Valley. Mom didn't like this and we agreed that this was only until Frank jr. finished school at Cortland State. She was leaving all her friends, that she had made all those years on Ridge Street, and I was parting with my friends at school, and would have to finish my 8th grade and start my high school freshman year at Spring Valley. I wasn't a happy camper either. Daddy was in a spot, and we knew it, and we all had to make the best of it. When dad remodeled the homestead, before George passed away, they added on a big room on the side of the house, not knowing what was going to happen. A good thing they did, now the downstairs apartment was three bedrooms, what we needed.

We moved and I transferred to the North Main Street Jr. High School which was only a short walk from Myrtle Avenue. I met some kids that I played base ball against, back when I played for Harry Jackson's Red Bird team at the Memorial Park. We became friendly, but it wasn't like my buddies in Pearl River. I would catch the bus and go down to P R on the week end nights, if something was going on , but mostly I stayed home with mom. She was a little depressed about the move; she never liked the homestead to begin with, and wasn't thrilled about living in a house that had anything to do with Mary Dawson, dad's mother, that never liked her from the beginning.

Like I said before, mom was a rock, and she sucked it up, she knew Frankie had to finish college. She knew dad was working hard to make the whole show go round and round. She was always looking out for me too, and if I needed a few bucks here and there, she'd slip me a couple and say, don't tell your father. This is from your 'best-est pal", and she was that, my whole life.

CHAPTER 15

We lived on Myrtle Ave. well into 1956, Dwight Eisenhower was the President of the UNITED STATES after Mr. Truman left office, and the country was rolling along fairly well. Eisenhower was in office, during and after the Korean War, and was faced with putting men coming home from the war, back to work. He started the INTERSTATE HIGHWAY SYSTEM, which meant more new roads, and many more new jobs, for these men and boost our economy. Work wise, everything was going pretty well. I even got a part time job in a pool parlor, in town, grooming tables and racking balls for the heavy betting pool players. They liked me and I liked the money.

Mom became good friends with the Sullivan family across the street, and after a while she wasn't so depressed. She looked forward to when Frankie would come home from school, for the holidays. It would give her a chance to cook a big meal, she was a fine cook, and every one of us told her so. Frank even brought his new girlfriend from college, home for Thanksgiving dinner.

THANKSGIVING and CHRISTMAS were big times for us. Frankie would come home, mom would cook and we would eat too much, of course, and we were happy. Dad had to get him another car to make it back to Cortland. Those two hundred and fifty mile trips, each way can make a good car, old quick. Dad got a good deal on 1951 mercury and Frank was back in business. It was a nice car and the payments weren't too bad, of course he lied to mom about that. He always wanted to make sure Frank had a safe ride, no matter what. Dad said he had a Rabbi at the bank, and he did, a fellow he went to school with, and could get a loan when he needed it. One thing about dad, he had good credit, and paid his bills on time and taught us to do the same.

Time was flying by and the winter of 1956 was ending and the winter of 1957 had begun. That January was cold and Frank said that they had so much snow in Courtland, this winter, that they ran out of places to put it all, and that they couldn't find six or seven cars buried under the snow until spring. He was busy playing basketball his final senior year, to worry about the snow. He also informed his mother that he had a new girl, and that this was the one. Wedding bells were in the future for sure, he said. Well mom got sad, her boy was getting ready to fly the nest, and she hadn't seen him that much during the summer time, with him playing basketball at Bear Mountain every summer, and playing softball at nights and weekends. She had missed his growing up years, but was glad that he'd grown to be a fine young man.

Mom always said, trust in GOD, HE will always be there for you, and she was right. While Frank was in his last year at Cortland, things started getting tight, money wise with dad. With the Mercury car payment, and all the bills, he was thinking of mortgaging the homestead. He talked it over with mom. Mommy told me about it and I told her to tell dad to use some of the money that Uncle George left to me, when he died. She knew that the chances of me going to college were poor; I did not like school that much and they both knew it. They also talked about selling the house. That's when mom got her brain storm,

She called her friend Gertrude, and told her to look in the local paper about any apartments for rent in Pearl River. She had already talked to Mrs. Sullivan, across the street, and asked if she knew anybody that would be interested in buying the homestead. Well the Sullivan's had a few bucks, and their son was getting married in the summer and they thought that it would be a great investment for the whole family, and the newlyweds would have an apartment to start off with, right across the street from his mother. Mommy did all this conniving behind dads back of course. She hopped on the bus to Pearl River, met her friend and they looked at two apartments, both on Central Avenue, in the middle of town. The one she picked wasn't going to be empty for two more months and that was perfect. She gave the owner of the building a deposit on it, and the deal was done. Now all she had to do was tell dad, and for him to get together with Mr. Sullivan, to buy the house.

Well for mom, the LORD did move in mysterious ways. She broke the news to dad. First I thought he was going to have a canary. After a short while, he combed down and thought it over. She told him that she didn't like it in this house, and in this town. She missed her friends from Ridge Street and she knew that Alvie, that's what she called me, missed his friends too. She also told him that his oldest son, Frank, had plans of getting married when he finished school. Mom hit him with this all at once, and like a general going to war, she went for the kill, and told him that the Sullivan's were ready to talk price on the house, and that she had put a deposit on an apartment already. He almost baulked, but then she sent in the clincher, and told him that she and I were going with, or without him. I told you, she was the family rock and when she put her foot down, that was it.

The Sullivan's bought the house, not for the price dad wanted, but at least he liked them, and he felt better knowing that the house went to friends. Now there was no worry about Frankie finishing school and we were getting ready to move back home. Mom was excited, and so was I. She called Gertrude and told her the good news. I helped mom pack up some boxes and dad set a few nights aside to paint the new place, to get it all ready. It turned out that dad knew the owner of the building and had done some plumbing work for him in the past. The man's name was Bill Rowan and he owned the bar on the ground floor of the building.

The apartment was a good size one, living room, kitchen and three bedrooms. We had to park in the back of the building. In a lot where the bar costumers parked. There was a back door that led to our hall way and stairs, up to the second floor. It was great, and the driveway to the lot was right next to the original Muddy Brook, the town was named after. We finally returned to where we belonged, PEARL RIVER, and mommy was happy at last. I got back into school and was with my old friends, some things had changed, the CAMPUS, across the street had a new owner ,Steve, a real nice guy, and he would remind us that we had to get back to school, and not be caught skipping. He was like a big brother to us all.

I wasn't doing to good in school, screwing off, missing classes and giving teachers a hard time. A lot of them had my brother in their classes and would compare me with him. He was a good student and I was the opposite. It was September of 1958; I was out for football and trying to make the team. All my friends were playing and I wanted to be there with them. This was not to be. I had gotten into some trouble in school, sent to the office where Uncle Ira, who was the assistant Principal, at that time, read me the riot act and tried to give me the good advice that I needed. Well I didn't listen to him, I got pissed off and went home and told mom that I had enough of school and I was quitting. She was not happy with me, and told me not to tell dad what had happened at school. A few days passed, I hadn't changed my mind and now I had to tell my father the bad news. Mom had fixed dinner and we sat down to the table and he asked me how things were going at school. I didn't lie to him, I told him that I quit, and he just looked at me. He said that he had heard that up at the paper store that morning and wanted to hear it from me. He said that he was disappointed, but if that's what I wanted to do, it was ok with him except for one thing. This is Thursday night, and you will have a job by Monday at dinner time, or we won't be expecting you at the dinner table that night. Dad didn't want me to become a bum, and told me that he didn't want any room and board from me, but he would not feed somebody that wouldn't go to work. Monday, at dinner time, we were sitting at the table and he asked me if I had a job, and I told him that I got one at Feisal's Express, moving furniture, forty hours a week. All he said to that was, 'let's eat'. We dropped it right there.

CHAPTER 16

By this time Frank had graduated from college and was looking for a teaching and coaching job. He found one at Park Ridge High, in NEW JRESEY, about six miles south of PEARL RIVER. He was not pleased with me, about quitting school, but did not break my chops to bad. I think mom told him to let it ride and cool it. I was dating a great girl in PARK RIDGE at that time, but it didn't turn into anything. She had a lot of problems with her mother and father. They were Catholic, and I was not, and that was the part that her mother didn't like, so the relationship ended, and we both moved on. We were both too young and it was just puppy love anyway.

Frankie got married to his girlfriend from college, Lynn, she came from LONG ISLAND, and that's where the wedding took place. They rented an apartment in PARK RIDGE, for about a year and then bought a house in Montvale N J., a nice little town close to the school, where they both worked. Lynn became pregnant soon after them moving to the house. This was the first of three children they were to have.

Frank wanted to become the coach that he idolized in school, Ira Shuttelworth, and he was on his way. I was taking a different road in my life. I had enough of moving furniture and was ready to move on. I had learned to drive a tractor trailer, but only being eighteen years old, no company would hire an inexperienced kid like me. A friend of my brother told me that where he worked, they were hiring helpers to deliver beer. This sounded pretty good. I put on my suit and tie and went to apply for a job. I was hired on the spot and could start right then and there. I took off my suit coat, my white shirt and tie and went to work on the beer truck as a helper. After being there two years, I took the warehouse job, unloading beer trailers from the brewery, and parking trailers in the yard, so they would be ready to go to the city for more beer, the following day.

I started bowling at the alleys in Nanuet NY. where I ran into a friend from school, Jeff Cole. We became good friends, actually best friends, he had friends that drank there and I became one of the crew of steady bar customers to hang out there. Jeff worked at a rubber stamp factory in SPRING VALLEY, and didn't much care for his job. We were both heavy drinkers at this time. He drank to forget his job, and

I drank because it was part of my job, and I liked it. While hanging out there, at the allies, I met my first wife, she was bowling with a team from Lederle Labs, where she worked, we started dating and things progressed from there. Jeff had met a girl there also, and we doubled dated a few times. Well things were going along fine and Sharan and I got engaged.

After the engagement, we had decided to wait a while. We had plans to make and wanted to do it right. Jeff and his girlfriend had a bad breakup and he decided to enlist into the Army. He went to boot camp at Fort Dix, in NEW JERSEY, and after that he was sent to Vietnam, where the war was still going on. It was 1961, and Nam was not the place to be. I was worried sick as was his mom and dad. I think it was a good move for him. I think he needed to get away, he was drinking a lot and I think the ARMY just might have saved his life. He did two, one year tours of duty there and decided to make the ARMY his carrier. He stayed in for over twenty years and retired a master sergeant. Thank GOD, he got home from Nam alive. So many of our young men, and woman gave their lives in that terrible war.

I had started playing softball for Reiss Beer Sale in the Sunday league in PEARL RIVER. A lot of the cops that made up the team were getting older and they needed some young blood to hold the team together. It was still a good league, a lot of young teams. It finally came to pass that REISS had to combine with another team, and that's when we formed a new team, MODREN AUTO BODY. Frankie was the pitcher and I was catching or playing first base. We had a lot of good players and won a few championships. This was a slow pitch league, and we had to form another fast pitch team, to play in a bunting and stealing league. This team was ANDY'S MENS WARE. Both these teams set many records, and won many tournaments in ROCKLAND COUNTY, during the 60's and 1970's.

I'm a senior citizen now, at the age of 69 years old and I look back at those years with fondness. I was fortunate to be affiliated with two of the best softball teams in the county, and to play with, and against some of the best players in the area. The best part of these years was that I was able to play with my hero, my older brother Frank. We played for these two teams almost twenty years.

After our engagement, Sharan and I made plans for our wedding. We were going to keep it a small affair, about sixty or seventy people at the most. By the time we made up the invitation list, it grew to almost one hundred people. We trimmed the list as much as we could, and sent out the invites. She picked out her gown, we found a reception restraint. We wanted to try to keep the cost down. We knew that her parents didn't have a lot of money. We all agreed these were the best plans and everything moved forward towards the big day in October. Something was wrong; I couldn't put my finger on it, until Sharan called me, and said that her mother would not let the marriage go through. I got in my car and went up to her house and walked into a hornets' nest. All I heard was that I wasn't any good and she was too young, and if I didn't get out of their house they were going to call the cops. They advised me that they never had any intention of paying for the wedding, which they waited until it would be too late and we would have to call the whole thing off. Well this changed a lot of things and we had to make some quick decisions. We only had three weeks to go until wedding day.

After a heated argument and me telling them what they could do with their wedding money, and a few other choice words. I asked Sharan what she wanted to do, did she want to get married to me, or did she want to stay here and be controlled by her mother. I wanted an answer from her, or I was leaving. She could come with me to our apartment, or we could call her dearest aunt and stay with her. She was very upset when we got to her aunt's house. She ended up staying there until our wedding day. Her mother and step father did not come to the wedding and I could have given a shit.

I was in a bind, I needed money fast to pay for this wedding. The only option I had was to sell my brand new Ford convertible, of which I owed money on. I had put a big down payment on the car and when I took it to the city to sell it, the bank got paid and we had about two thousand left over. I was still short two thousand. I went to the friend that my father had at our bank and floated a quick loan, mom cosigned for me and now all I had to do was get some kind of car so I could get back and forth to work. I picked up an old Chevy, in very good shape, about seven years old. Thank GOD that I had a good job at the beer distributor and Sharan had hers at Lederle. We were all set, her aunt was great and helped her with the last minute arrangements and I made sure everybody was going to get paid. I gave all the checks to be paid out to my brother and the day we got married I only had eighteen bucks in my pocket of a rented tux. No lie.

Apparently I had underestimated my mother in-law before the wedding. I can see now that she had no intention for her daughter to leave home, and get married. She had played her part very well, thinking that if she waited until the last minute we would have to call off the wedding, that we didn't have the money needed to go through with it. Well she was wrong, as she was many other times in our marriage. This was a big warning for me, and it looked like I was going to have the same problem, that my mother had with Mary Dawson. Intimation is a great tool, if you know how to work it. Sharan was definitely intimidated by her mother and this I would find out down the road through our marriage. I knew that I was not liked by her mother, and the feelings were mutual, I slept very well and could have given a shit what she thought. I've prided myself about one thing, if someone shits on you once, you don't give them another chance to do it again. Looking back, in the long run, she won out with her daughter, but not with me.

Soon after our marriage we found out that we were going to have a baby. This was great news. Even though we were in somewhat of a hole, money wise, from the wedding, we started to make plans for late June or July, for the new arrival. This news didn't soften up any feelings from my in-laws in the least, as far as I was concerned. Sharan was getting large and on July 19th we haled ass for the hospital in Suffern NY. I was not doing very well. I was worried all to hell and praying at the same time.

I was sitting in the waiting room for hours. Other fathers were coming and going whenever the phone would ring. They would call from upstairs, when your baby arrived. Well, I waited and waited. I really started to get worried and then out of the blue, my father arrived. He said that he remembered how he had felt, when I and Frankie were born, and thought he'd come and sit with me. He exclaimed that sometimes it can take a long time, and for me to relax. Easy for him to say. We waited over fifteen hours, and then the phone finally rang for me. I went up stairs and saw my son for the first time. I was scared, the baby looked like he was light blue and his head came almost to a point and I could see all the blue vanes in his body. I thought I was going to faint until the doctor came out and told me everything went fine. Just a little longer then he expected. He put my mind at ease when he told me that every baby looks like that, minutes after they are born, but he was perfect. We didn't call her parents when we started for the hospital, so out of kindness I called them and let them know that they had a grandson and that Brian was born early in the morning on the 20th of July. I will never forget that day, or the feeling that came over me when I first saw him. Any man who has become a father can relate to what I was feeling and how proud I was of my wife. We went home to our apartment in Nanuet, and I got my first lesson on changing diapers and heating formula. Of course I was handing out cigars to my friends at work and the softball team as well. We were happy in our small apartment, but things started to change.

CHAPTER 17

Mom and dad were still living in the apartment above the bar when Mr. Rowan informed them that he wanted to sell the building, and wanted to give dad enough time to make a move if they wanted to. Mom decided that there was another place that her and Gertrude had looked at years before, and see if was for rent. The building was owned by a local construction company that dad knew of and he went to check on the availably of any apartments in the building. Well it seemed that mom and GOD were on the same track once again. The apartments in the building were just done over and there were two for rent and mom could have her choice. The building was just up Central Avenue, a block away from where the presently lived. They took the biggest place and mom was quite happy. The Braunsdorf Park was just across the street, where she would meet Gertrude, sit in the shade, or go across the street to the coffee shop for some ice cream. It was closer to the Grand Union store, In the middle of town, for her shopping.

The apartment was good for mom, but not so good for dad. It was close to Oakley's paper store for the paper and cigarettes but it was sixteen steps up the stairs, and dad's lungs were getting bad from smoking those Old Gold cigarettes all those years. He was still working at the State Hospital; he had become the foreman of the plumbing shop years earlier, while Frank Jr. was still in college. They were doing ok and were living a quiet life. Dad wasn't well and finally stopped working his side jobs. He would stop and see Mr. Ablondi, at the bar, to say hello to his old friends. He would park his car around the back, on Ridge Street, so if mom was sitting in the park, she wouldn't see that he was having a beer. Like she couldn't tell if he had a beer or two. Ha!!

Well the baby was getting pretty big. We had noticed that his right foot was flopped over to the outside. We became concerned and took him to an orthopedic specialist. He said that Brian's foot was growing crooked and we had to put his feet into a special brace and that he would have to keep the brace on twenty hours a day. That was easier said than done. Brian hated that brace. He was six months old and would scream and cry when he had the brace on. When we took it off for the four hours he was fine, but trying to get it back on was a trip. It tore my heart out sometimes to have to do that to my son, but the doctor said that it was working and that his foot would be normal in a few more months. We went through two cribs; he would raise his both feet in that brace and come down on the rails and just splinter the sides.

Living in Nanuet was fine with us. I joined the fire department and our apartment was close to everything. I had joined the Teamsters Union at my job, and that meant that I would have benefits for my family, and a retirement plan later on down the road. Then we got another surprise, we were pregnant again. So much for that rule , no sex for six weeks before or six weeks after giving birth. Well, what can I say, we were happy about the news and we were going to have to make a few adjustments. We had an opportunity to buy our first house and we did. It was a small, two bedroom house, on Lexow Avenue in Nanuet, not far from the fire house. It was pretty cheap, and we could just about afford it, the payments were less than the rent we were paying on the apartment.

Well along came Robyn Dawson, eleven months to the day, after Brian was born. We didn't have to wait too long for Robyn to arrive. She was eager to see the world and on June 20th, Fathers Day, two hours after we got to the hospital, she was born. I had envisioned another long wait, but GOD had different plans, and the phone rang, and I left the other guys in the waiting room, instead of me being left. She was beautiful then as she is today. We all went home to our little house, and we already had the dresser draw ready for Robyn in our room. By this time Brian had his own room, and there would be room for another crib when Rob outgrew her draw. Brian was all excited with the new baby, and confused at the same time. He had been out of the foot brace about a month before we brought Robyn home.

Brian's foot healed perfectly, straight as an arrow. The doctor said that he didn't think he wouldn't have any further problems with the foot at all. Soon after we moved into the house, and everything seemed to be going our way, the bottom fell out. We had a labor strike where I worked and I was out of work for nine weeks. Talk about getting into a hole. I picked up a few jobs, here and there, but not the steady money that I was making at the beer distributor. They settled the strike and we went back to work. We didn't get anything that we had struck for and it all seemed like a total waist. I became depressed with my job and decided that I had to make a change. When I talked to a friend of mine, he told me that a fellow he knew was a business agent for the Teamsters, and that he was looking for tractor trailer drivers for steady job. I met with this man and decided to take a chance and make this big move. I was leaving the beer job, where I was making $135.00 a week, which in 1964, wasn't bad money and going to a trailer job in heavy construction, making $250.00 a week. I already had a Teamster's book; all I had to do was transfer the book to the Teamsters local that was on the job. One problem, I would not have any medical insurance on my family until I accumulated one thousand hours of work. So we sweated this time out. Thank GOD, the construction project that I worked on lasted almost three years. By this time we had the hospital coverage, and I had built up a reputation as a good driver, and found steady work in the summer months. I liked the Teamsters Local I transferred too.

I was out of work a few winters but I was always able to find odd jobs to make ends meet. During this time Sharan became pregnant again and we had to make a move to a bigger house. We found one right around the corner from ours on Fruind Drive. We bought the house; it had three bedrooms and would be just right for our new addition arriving in the winter. On Valentine's Day that year Eileen was born and we didn't need a dresser draw for her. We had enough room, the two girls would have their own bedroom and Brian would have his. The world was perfect, or so I thought at the time. I did a lot of work on the newer house. I put in a big patio, an above the ground pool for the kids, big and small. I also made a den and did some work in the basement and garage. I was pretty active in the Nanuet Fire Company and I was playing a lot of softball with my brother and for the fire house team. Work was plentiful in those years; I was good at what I did and never turned down a driving job and took all the overtime that I could get. I also never got fired from a job and the heads of my Local Union noticed these things and made me a shop steward, which is in charge of all the drivers on all of the jobs, I would have in the future. This meant extra money per week, and that I would be the last man on the job site until that job was completed. This was the career that I had made for myself and I had built my reputation on being fair to the men that worked under me, and to the companies that I worked for, over thirty four years in my Teamsters Local Union, and retired from there in 1998 with a full pension.

While at Fruind Dr., Brian and Robyn had started school and took the bus every morning right out in front of the house. They were gone a good part of the day and Sharan would take Eileen with her and go up to see her mother. This apparently was a steady thing each day, or at least three times a week. There still was no love lost between me and her mother. I did not see what was happening, that my wife was being, once again intimidated by her mother. I was busy working and playing ball and didn't notice that she and the children didn't have the time to come to the games. Now that I look back, I should have noticed this, and other things, but did not. After a while, a long while, like a puzzle, all the pieces were coming together.

My father's health was failing. He had built up a lot of sick time at the State Hospital and was forced to take this time off and relax. His lungs were shutting down. His breathing was becoming worse, and it became more difficult for him to climb the stairs to the apartment on Central Avenue. It became evident that those stairs were going to kill him. They would have to move to a ground floor unit or else.

CHAPTER 18

Dad had used up his sick time from his job. With the doctor's recommendation, he decided to retire. Brother Frank and I had talked it over and told mom that we had to look for a place for them to live.

Frankie had his own problems with his first marriage. It ended in a bitter separation and divorce. While separated from his wife, he stayed with mom and dad. He had taken a new coaching job in a bigger high school, further south in NEW JERSEY. He had three children from his first marriage, one boy, the oldest, and two girls. After a short time, he and this woman he had met at the same school, dated and ended up getting married. They lived close to the school, where they both taught and soon after the wedding he had informed us all that a baby was on the way. Well he had his hands full. They had an apartment in her family's big house and down the road there were more children added to the Dawson, second family. All toll, Frank had six children from his two marriages. Two boys and four girls. The children from the first marriage, stayed with their mother, who remarried to a nice guy.

The fellow that Lynn married had three sons himself and his wife had passed away. They only lived a few houses away from each other and got to know each other through friends. Anyway, now they were together, and had six children to raise. Frank made sure that he could see them and tried to have some kind of relationship with them. They had to move to Columbus Ohio, because of the step-fathers job and this made it hard on the relationship between the three Dawson kids and their father. This move, plus many other problems between them and their father and his new family took a heavy toll down the road. A lot of things could have been done and said to the children, differently and being eight hundred miles away from them was a said factor for him and them.

Frank and I talked over mom and dad's problem. We knew that He couldn't bring them down to live with them in Garfield NJ. Mom would not have anything to do with that. My house was too small and I had no room to build on to it. There weren't any ground floor apartments available in PEARL RIVER to be had. I talked it over with my wife and we decided to look for a bigger house that we could make an apartment for my mother and father. Frank and I agreed to this and we together would do whatever we had to do to make it work. It wasn't easy; first I had to sell my house on Frieund Dr. so I would have the money to put down on another house for all of us. Sharan needed to look for a house that would fit our needs and one that we could afford. After a few weeks, she found a house in PEARL RIVER. The house was a big bi level and it was more than we could afford on our own. I took Mom and Dad to look over the house, which was vacant, and to see if there was enough room for a one bedroom apartment down stairs for them to live. I would have to make one of the garages into a bedroom and make a small kitchen and make the bath room bigger. They agreed that it would work. It was on the ground floor and they would have a little patio outside the door, to sit in the shade. It looked great. I would start thinking what I needed to do, to make over the new bedroom and all the rest. First things first, I had to sell my house. This is where it gets tricky. The owners of the house in PEARL RIVER were holding to their price and I was trying to barter them down. It worked; I got them to where we could afford the house, with a little left over. One problem, they wanted to close on the house with in thirty days. This I could not do. I had no money. All my money was in my home in Nanuet, and all I had in the bank was about two thousand dollars. I needed at least ten thousand more dollars and a good banker to close the deal. Well it was crunch time. Time to get the balls out of the closet. I called big brother Frank and told him where we were at on the house deal and told him that I had an idea, but needed his help to pull it off. I had just started a big job, a power house, that I was going to be on for at least three years and I would be making good money. I told him this and told him that I needed ten thousand dollars cash to put down on the house and I needed a good banker, if he knew any, to swing the deal for us. This is where it got sticky and everybody was sweating for a while.

Frank told me that I was crazy, which I probably was, but we had to take a chance for dad's sake, if not for any other reason. He didn't have ten thousand dollars. I asked him if he could get it from his father-in-law, who was pretty well loaded? He said no way, but there might be a way with somebody else. I was open to whatever he had in mind. There was this guy that his father-in-law knew where we could find the money, for 1% on the money borrowed, per month until the whole amount was paid off. It would cost me one hundred dollars a month just to borrow the ten grand. I would put this in my savings account, giving me a total of over twelve thousand dollars. Frankie had a friend that he knew from high school that was a loan officer in a savings and loan bank and I went to meet him and fill out the mortgage loan papers. Well, he thought that there shouldn't be a problem; I had twelve thousand in the bank, over thirty thousand equity in the house that I was selling and a good job and good credit through the years. I looked like a done deal. Now I was the owner of two houses, with two mortgages, of which I couldn't afford and a shy lark in NEW JERSEY who I owed ten thousand dollars too and was paying him one hundred dollars a month interest until it was paid off. WONDERFUL. It gets better than that. The house didn't sell in Nanuet, and was vacant for over a year. Well my friend GOD, was looking out for me and answered my prayers. The house sold and I made more on it then I had planned. The apartment was made at the new house for mom and dad and they had moved in two months after we bought it.

With the house in Nanuet sold I could pay off the loan shark in NJ. Frank could breathe a little easier. The ten thousand dollar debt was done and it had cost me about twelve hundred dollars to swing the deal. Dad was breathing a little better. The kids started in the PEARL RIVER school system and went to Evens Park grammar school, only two blocks away from the new house on White Avenue. Thank GOD I was working steady on the new power house job, so that I would be able to pay both mortgages for two houses. Once again, my friend upstairs was looking out for me and mom. We did the best we could to help dad, but in the end it just wasn't enough. He lasted about two years. The lack of clean oxygen getting into his body and lungs was making him delirious, carbon-deoxidize was building up and his brain and balance would go hay wire. We had to put him into the same hospital where we had put Uncle Giggy, Summit Park, in Pomona NY. Dad passed away in 1975, he was only 68 years old. A combination of hard work all his life, problems with his heart and of course smoking four packs of cigarettes a day, which gave him an acute form of enphysima. His lungs simply could not hold the air he was breathing in, causing his heart to fail.

We laid dad to rest with the rest of the Dawson family at the New Hempstead Cemetery, next to his older brother Bill. Now all the brothers were together with their mother and father. Mom stayed at White Avenue about another year, but was not happy. One day she called me down to her apartment for a talk. She said that there were things going on that I should know about, that my wife was hardly ever home, and neither were the kids. She had heard screaming on the telephone for hours on end. She also knew that we were arguing a lot and that things weren't right with Sharan and me. She was right, a lot of things were wrong. I had given my wife basically a free rein to run the house. We had a joint checking account and the same savings account also. Working at the power house, I was making between eight hundred and one thousand dollars a week, big money for 1975. Sometimes I would even make more than that, if we had to work on Sundays, ten and twelve hours a day, I could make up to two thousand for the week. This money I thought was going to paying the bills for the house, car payment and utility bills. I came to find out that the phone bills were ranging between two hundred and three hundred and fifty dollars a month. Mostly overtime calls to her mother's house. To say that I was mad to find these things out was an understatement. I questioned my wife about these things, and couldn't get any direct answers. All I got was bull shit. Well I did a lot more checking on our finances and found that our checking account was close to empty. I was making great money; she was driving a school bus, and we were broke.

I could see that I wasn't getting any straight answers as to where all the money had gone, and to this day I have my own ideas but I can't prove a thing. I knew in my heart, what was going on. The straw that broke the camel's back was the morning we woke up and somebody stole our brand new 1973 Pontiac station wagon out of our driveway. I called the police, they came to the house and filled out the report and left. About an hour later, the police called, they found the car, it was repossessed and it was sitting at the bank in NEW JERSEY, where I had borrowed the money for the car. Come to find out that the payments were four months overdue and had called rapidly and spoke to Mrs. Dawson about the problem, and apparently were getting the same bull shit answers I was getting. Well I had to float a quick loan from a friend, to bail the car out and also had to pay an extra one hundred and fifty dollars towing fee. Things were not good at White Avenue. I tried not to bring this crap up in front of the kids; they knew a lot more than I did, apparently. It didn't do any good talking about it anymore, I couldn't get any truth. I was being lied to and deceived too. I was at the end of my rope. I was going to make a move but I didn't know which way to go. I told mom that we would look for another place for her. She was not happy in this house and knew what was going on. She had seen all this before, years ago with dad, him being dominated by his mother, Mary Dawson, the same as Sharan was being controlled by her mother, because of the bad feelings that she still had towards me.

CHAPTER 19

I found Mom a nice little one bedroom apartment on the corner of Franklin Avenue and Ridge Street in our old neighborhood. She was back with some of her old friends. There was a little deli across the street and the candy store, next door. One thing about Mom, she was a collector. You wouldn't believe the crap that I moved from place to place over the years. New dresses that still had the price tags on them, coats the same way, and gobs of knick knacks by the box full. This was her thing, rummage sales and five and ten stores. If it was on sale, Mom had it whether she needed it or not, but she was my "best est-pal" and whatever it took to make her happy, was okay with me and Frankie.

There wasn't an evil bone in Mom's body. She wouldn't let anybody shit on her and like me you didn't get a second shot at her. This is why she wanted to move from White Avenue. She knew that she was not wanted there and she knew that I was going to have a problem with my wife and she felt it would be better for me if she was out of there. She was right, as usual. The fighting and hollering didn't stop, the kids were suffering through the whole thing and it was time.

I wrote my best friend Jeff, who was stationed in Oregon and told him of my problems and what I had intended to do. He called me right away to give me support. I could always count on Jeff. He was always there for me and me for him. That's the way it was, we were like brothers and still are. Frank knew something was up when Mom told him that she was moving. He had his own problems and couldn't help me with mine. I was the only person that had to make the hardest decision of my life. I was going to leave my children with their Mother and move out of the house. This was not easy for me and it took a lot of thought before I did it. It was for the best. The screaming and hollering would stop. They would still be in school in Pearl River.

I couldn't stop what other family members were going to tell them about me, when I left. I could only hope that someday I would be able to explain to them why this had happened. I knew that I was going to be the bad guy here, but I wasn't going to put the kids into a tug of war between their Mother and me for their affections. They were only still in grammar school and too young to understand what was going on. I'm sure that I was going to be the bad guy, so be it. I would be honest with them when the time came to answer whatever questions they had when they were grown. Life is hard, and marriage is hard too. To stay married you need love and respect for each other. Cheating, lying and deceiving one another only lead to separation. You have to pull together, when one pulls and the other doesn't, this doesn't work.

Don't get me wrong, my wife wasn't the only person at fault here. I had my faults, I knew that I was drinking too much, away playing softball a lot, but I was also working a lot of hours, making good money that I thought was going into the bank and it was paying the bills. I was about to make the most painful decision of my life. Leaving my children. I told my wife that I would continue to pay the mortgage and taxes on the house so the kids could stay in school in PEARL RIVER and she was going to take care of the rest. I was leaving. I packed a few things and moved in to a hotel in Nanuet. It was a one room, dirty place and wasn't what I had wanted for myself. It would have to do for a while. I had met a woman while I was in turmoil with my wife. We were not intermit, just friends. I found that I could talk to her about my problems at home and she had similar ones of her own. She was bartending in a bar that Jeff and I use to hang out in and I found myself going there a lot to see her. I was at a very low time in my life, couldn't get my kids out of my mind and hoped that someday they would understand why I left them. I must have hurt them very much. I stayed about four weeks in the hotel and decided that there had to be a better place to live. I checked around and found nothing any cleaner or suitable. Well Sue, the woman I had been talking too about my troubles, had an extra room at her house and offered it to me and I would pay her rent. It was clean and she said that she could use the extra money. She was a single mother and it would pay for her babysitter, while she went to work.

The house was in WEST NYACK NY. It was a small, three bedroom house, more like a cottage. Sue had a three year old daughter, a very pretty little girl and we liked each other right off. I would check in with my children every week, they seemed cold towards me. They were not happy with me leaving them but it was for the best all around. Sharan was still hostel towards me, but that wasn't anything new. I use to tell her when we were fighting that you never miss what you have, until you don't have it anymore. This is true! I missed my kids, but I did not miss her, and all the fighting.

The power house job was done and I was moving on to another job after the winter break. I was collecting unemployment insurance during the winter and money was short. I kept paying for the house and paying my own rent to Sue. It was slim, but we made it through that winter. I was getting complaints about how much the bills were at the house and how much the food and the utilities cost. All the things that I had thought the big money I was making the previous year, was paying for. The goose that laid the golden egg had left the coop. I often wonder about all that money. I knew where it went, and my ex-wife, and someone else knew also. As they say, that's water under the bridge and it was time to move on. Sue and I were getting to be more than just friends. I found in her what I didn't have with my wife, honesty. We didn't lie to each other and we made no excuses for our past life and were happy in our relationship, at least for a while.

Time was passing by quickly and I had started another job in the county and it would last only a year or a little more. Brian was in his senior year at PEARL RIVER HIGH and doing well. He told me that he wanted to go to college and take up animal husbandry. He had a horse for a little while and that's what he wanted to do. Breed animals. By this time Sharan and I decided to sell the house and she wanted to move up to her mother's house in Suffern. That was not a real big surprise to me at all. We sold the house, and after a little argument about on how the money would be split up from the sale, we parted and let's say it was not a hand shaking and wish you well goodbye.

It was the summer when we sold the house. Robyn had her senior year to go in school and wanted to stay in PEARL RIVER with her friends. She was on the track team, and wanted to graduate there. I talked it over with Sue and we agreed that she could ride down to school when she dropped off Loni, her daughter, to the sitters house, and pick them both up after she finished work. It looked like it would work out fine. Robyn and Sue got along fine and Robyn was starting to realize that her daddy was not the bastard that some people made him out to be. Sue and I were living in an apartment in WEST HAVERSTRAW NY. At that time is when Robyn started to live with us. It was becoming quite evident that the place was too small for all of us and that we would have to make a move. We did, we rented a house in NAURASHAUN, a small area of PEARL RIVER. It was a big house.

Soon after moving to Lark Street in Naurashaun, I went to visit mom, down at her place at Franklin Avenue. It was a good thing that I went, she was ill and disorientated. It looked like she had not taken her medicine and that she had not eaten for a while. At first she didn't recognize me and I got scared. Well I wasn't taking any chances, I called her doctor and he told me that he was calling the ambulance and wanted her in the hospital right away. He had seen her two days before and told her that she was losing too much weight and was concerned about her. Apparently she blew him off and told him it was nothing to worry about. He took her blood for testing the day she was there and when his office called her that afternoon, they got no answer. They wanted to tell her that her sugar count was too low and that needed to take her medicine. She never got the message. GOD was once again looking out for her, and sent me to visit her. She was not eating properly, the milk in the fridge was sour, and bread was moldy. For a woman that lived on corn flakes, bananas and milk and cold cut sandwiches, this was telling me that she hadn't had anything to eat in days. I called my brother and told him that we were taking her to the hospital and I would get in touch with him later and give him the scoop.

We got to the hospital none too soon. Once there, mom went into shock and they rushed her into the intensive care unit. She was in tough shape. I was a nerves wreck, and all I could do was prey and that's what I did. The LORD and I were not strangers.

After many hours of waiting, Frankie arrived and we met with the doctor and he filled us in. mommy was very sick and right now she was becoming stable. He told us that he feared that she had cancer. He wasn't sure where it was and that he wanted to do more tests, but when she got stronger. She was severely dehydrated and needed fluids and food the build herself up before he would go forward with the testing. We had a good doctor and went along with his recommendations. Mom was in there for about two weeks, the rest did her good. Her med's been stable and before the doctors cut her lose from the hospital, he wanted to meet me there. We talked and he informed me that mom had a tumor with-in her intestinal tract and it needed to be removed soon. He wanted to make sure that she was strong enough before he went ahead with the operation. He also told us that this was a life threatening type of tumor and must be removed, there were no options. I told mom what the story was and all she said to me was that "we will trust in GOD, HE will take us through it". The rock of the family was cracking, but she was not down and out. She had her faith in the LORD and that was fine with Frankie and me. We told the doctor to go ahead with the operation while she was here and if he thought she was stable enough. And he said that he wanted to wait a few more days, take a few more finial tests and call in another special cancer surgeon to assist him with the operation. During this time Frank and I discussed mom coming home with me and Sue at Lark Street. This was fine with him. We would tell mom after the operation was over.

CHAPTER 20

They were going ahead with the operation the next day at seven am. I called work and got the day off and made sure that I was at the hospital early enough to see mom. I got there just in time; they were getting her ready to go down to the operating room. She looked up at me and said for me not to worry and she would see me when she woke up. I held back my tears and kissed her on the far-head and told her that I loved her. She said, I know, and they rolled her away.

I went to the waiting room and sat for what seemed like hours and hours. After about an hour and a half, the doctor appeared, he came over to me and I feared the worst. He said that mom was resting in the recovery room, not awake just yet. He explained to me that they had opened mom up and found that the tumor was a large one and that it was involved into her stomach and her liver and some of her intestines. He then said that they could not cut it out, that it was too massive and that if they attempted to do so, mom would not survive the surgery.

I asked the doctor what the bottom line was with mom's condition, what would happen next? He told me that the situation was terminal and that mom had between three and six months to live. He said that we had a few options. One was to put mom in a nursing home. Another was to take her home and get a nurses aid for about four hours a day to make sure she took her meds and to bathe her and fix her food.

I told the doctor that I was not putting my mother into a nursing home, no way, and that we would go with the second option. He said that he would set things in motion and that mom could come home in a few days. When mom woke up, Frankie had arrived and we filled her in a little and told her that the doctor said everything would be ok. No sense telling her the truth while she was in the hospital. We told her that she had to come home with me because the new medicine was to strong and she needed to be watched closely. We also told her that she was going to have a nurse's aid come in every day, give her the meds, and make her some food. You couldn't bull shit mom for long, she knew that something was up. When she got to our house, a hospital bed, which the doctor ordered, had already arrived and was all set up in her own privet room. She had a half bath next to her room and was easy for her to get to. She was not bed-ridden yet. She could get around pretty good, make her own tea and make her favorite, corn flakes and a banana. The day after she got home, a call came from a Miss Joan Davis; she was the aid that the doctor ordered for mom.

Miss Davis needed directions on how to get to our house. I told her and she said that she would come over the next day which was Saturday and wanted us to be there so she could meet us and go over things that she was going to do for mom. Come to find out that Miss Davis, a black woman, was the sister of a fellow that Frankie and I played softball against from Nyack. Teddy Davis was the manager of an all black team called CHIC-N-CHARLIE'S. They had a very good team and we lost a few games to them. Well Joan and mom hit off from the word go. They talk up a storm; mom had a lot of clothes that she gave to Joan to take over to her church, new shoes, gloves and all sorts of things that could be used by some poor folks. There was no color thing with mom, Joan could have been purple or pink, made no difference to mom, and when mom liked you, you had a friend for life. They took to each other like a duck takes to water. Sue was also a big factor in taking care of mom. She would shop for her and fix her dinner and do a lot of little things for her. They became friends, and Loni, Sue's daughter liked to play dress-up with mom. Mom had a lot of fake jewelry and some big hats and she would put make-up on Loni. They had a ball. Loni and mom were good company for each other after she got home from school. Joan Davis even joined in the play. This made a hard time in my mother's life much easier. I would come home from work and they would be sitting on the floor in the living room, playing make-up. I said to mom, how about a beer. She looked at me and said, why not. I went to the fridge and got two beers and we sat there and drank them.

After the first two beers were gone we had two more and then a third. Mom was feeling pretty good. She said to me that she was worried about her sugar count. I told her not to worry; Joan would give her, her meds in the morning. She had some dinner with Sue and me and went into her room and went to sleep and slept like a baby the whole night through. I told mom the next day what the doctor had told me about the tumor and how bad it was. She just looked at me and said that she knew that she had spoken to him before she left the hospital. You couldn't bull-shit mom. Then she said that GOD would take care of her and for me not to worry. Then my pal said, let's have a beer, and we had two and then two more. She loved her beer.

While we were enjoying our beers, big brother came to the house to see his mother. He saw that she had a beer and wanted to speak to me outside. We went out and he said to me that he was worried about mom's sugar and the beer. I said, shit Frank, what do you think is going to kill her first, sugar diabetes or the malignant tumor in her belly. He saw my point, and I told him that if she wanted a beer, she was getting a beer or two or whatever. Mom was up to about three and sometimes four beers a day. This was fine with me. Between the drugs and the beer, she was sleeping better then she had in years. I would go past her room at night and hear her saying her prayers, asking her LORD that she not be a burden to her sons, that she loved her boys and that she would miss them but she was ready when HE was, to take her.

Mom loved all her grandchildren, all nine of them, but I think that she had a special feeling for Robyn. She felt that Robyn was a lot like her. She was strong in one way and considerate of others, as long as they did not try to screw with her. She saw a lot of me in Robyn too; she was truthful, always ready to help you if she could. Robyn would stop in to her room to see if nanny needed anything or just to say hello. She was taking the school bus along with Loni every day, thou they went to different schools. Brian was in collage at Delhi, up state NY. He would only come home on holidays or spring break.

I noticed that mom had slowed down on having her beers during the day and had a meeting with MS. Davis. She told me that she noticed that mom was slipping into deep sleeps during the day and that her apatite was off quite a bit. She also told Joan that the pain was increasing and that she needed more Demerol, to ease it. I told Joan to call the doctor for further instructions about increasing the meds. She did this, and told me that I had to call the doctor's office when I got home from work. I talked to Dr. Chang and he advised me that I should consider putting mom into a nursing home that he thought that she was slipping and that she may not last much longer. I gave him the same answer that I gave him the first time he had mentioned a nursing home. NO WAY!!!. If mom was going to die, she was going to die with the family that she loved around her, not strangers in a nursing home. He said that he would instruct Ms. Davis to increase to meds.

Mom was not in a coma, but she wasn't wide awake either. The doctor increased the meds and changed the Demerol to Morphine. He said that this is what she would need to stop the pain completely. Joan was an angel with mom and took real good care of her. Some people have a gift to work with the dying and Joan had that gift. I had just got home from work and Joan came to me and told me that the end was near. I went into mom's room and sat by her bed and Joan left the room. I bent over and kissed mom on the for-head, she opened her eyes, I could tell that she was out of it somewhat. She smiled at me and said, HY PAL. I held her hand and cried as she went to sleep and went to the GOD that she loved and trusted.

CHAPTER 21

I was a wreck; I was crying and shaking all at the same time. I couldn't believe that she was gone. She would be out of my life forever I composed myself the best I could. Joan asked if there was anything that she could do. I told her no, she said that we had to call the doctor's office and let them know that mom had passed. She did this and then she called the funeral parlor for me and informed them that the doctor was notified so they would be able to pick mom up. Joan was great, she saw that I was torn up and she just jumped in and did what needed to be done. I pulled myself together the best I could and called Frankie. He answered the phone and when I told him that mom had passed, the phone went silent and then I could tell that he was sobbing and crying .After a few minutes, he got back on the phone and said that he had to call me back in a little while. I could feel his pain and I broke down again myself. I went back to mom's room and held her hand until they came for her.

The funeral was tough; thank GOD that Sue was there to hold me together. Brian came home from college and most of the family was there. A lot of mom's friends from Ridge Street were there also. They all shared a lot of memories through the years. The day of the burial was the toughest of all. I was weeping by myself and my brother went to the casket, leaned in and kissed his mother a final good bye. I went to him and we held each other with our grief. It was the saddest day of both of our lives.

We took mom to the family plot at New Hempstead Cemetery and interned her atop her mother's grave, as to her wishes. This is where my ashes will be spread when it's time for me to meet our GOD and I will be with her forever. They say that time heals all wounds, this is true and I was wounded deeply when she died. It has taken a long time for me to heal but as in life we have to go forward and put the past where it belongs. Memories are a wonderful thing; they last forever and can never be taken away. This is the thing I have all to myself, the memory of the most wonderful woman and mother in the world. I never knew her to be mean, or say a bad word about anyone. She took care of her father, brothers, husband and her two sons which were her life. This was a very special person. All her friends felt the same way about Anna and told me that she would be truly missed. I know that she was the reason that Frank and I grew up to be strong and caring men, and the values that she taught us will remain with us forever.

I grieved for a long time after mom passed. I was drinking too much and I know that my mood was bad most of the time. I kept in touch with my brother who was going through the same problems that I was having. Mom was our foundation, the blocks that we built our lives around and now she was gone. We had to rebuild our selves and get on with our lives with our families. That's what we did. Robyn graduated from high school and told me that she wanted to go to college at Southern Connecticut University. She could have had a partial scholarship to another school but she wanted to go where a few of her friends were going. This was going to be tight; Brian had one more year at Delhi and with Robyn going to college that meant that I would be paying two schools at the same time. Things were going to get tough around the Dawson house. Lot of hot dogs, lots of spaghetti diners. Oh well, thank GOD I rat hold the money from the sale of the house with Sharan. I was working steady and Sue was working too and she always carried her own weight with the house expenses. Loni was in school and we didn't need a sitter for her anymore, that's what mom and Joan Davis did for us when Loni got off the school bus, but now they were both gone. We were lucky, Loni was a good kid and did her homework when she got home and kept herself busy until we got home from work. Robyn would fill in as a sitter too, before she left for college, they became very close and were like real sisters. Robyn and her real sister Eileen did not get along that well. Eileen was a hard girl to figure out.

I know that she didn't care for me, but I don't know why she felt that way.

I believe that Eileen was influenced by her Grandmother, who had no love for me in the first place. I just couldn't compete with all the lies, either about me or to me. It got so I couldn't tell the good lies from the bad ones. Forget about telling the truth, that wasn't happening with Eileen. I tried to help her once, she was Baker Acted and called me from the mental clinic, to come and get her out. I couldn't do this because once you are charged with this; you must stay in the clinic for forty eight hours and then be evaluated before they will let you go. I went to see her and she seemed to want to have a relationship with me after all these years. It had been about fifteen years since we had even spoken. I guess I took the bait, her Mother said that she couldn't do anything for her and her Grandmother did not want her back in her house and had an order of protection against her. She had threatened her with harm. I agreed to help her. I found a room for her in Nyack; I paid the rent on the room for two months and gave her one hundred and fifty dollars to get some food and whatever. I knew that this wasn't going far and I was going for more money down the line.

I told Eileen that I would continue to help her as long as there were no lies between us. I hate a liar and I would not tolerate that anymore. Well this didn't last long.

One lie led to another lie and after a short while I realized this is the way that she faces life. I was being used and I told her so and she said that was tough shit and I could go to hell. That was it for me.

For the most part, we were done. I've seen her very few times since and we haven't talked to each other in years. I stopped sending birthday or Christmas cards long ago.

Sue, Loni and I stayed at Lark Street for a while after Mom passed. Both Brian and Robyn were in college and the holidays were coming up and they would be home for Christmas. They were both doing well in school or so I thought. After Mom left us, Sue and I would take Loni to see her Grandmother in Oceanside Long Island on the weekends and stay over and come home on Sunday nights. Sue's Mother Mavis and I were great friends; she and I even became partners on a thirty foot boat, which we kept at the marina a few blocks from her house. Mavis loved the boat, she would clean it and we would go out for the whole weekend on it. It was the winter now and boat was in dry dock and she was getting ready for next season. Christmas was over and the kids came home soon after for spring break. It was time to write the checks out for the rest of the college year for both of them. It was pretty tight and Brian had to get a student loan to finish up and graduate. He knew that I was squeaking by and got his loan.

Robyn on the other hand gave me the big surprise of the New Year. After she returned to Southern Connecticut University and I had written out the check of twenty eight hundred dollars and had already sent it to the school, this was for her last semester of the year. She then advised me that she was quitting school. The reason, the boy that she had a crush on was going with another girl. Come to find out that this is why she went to this school in the first place he had been I her class at Pearl River High School and this was why she had turned down a partial scholarship to another school. Oh, Well? Of course southern Connecticut did not send me back the money, no refunds!!.

Robyn decided to get away after that and took a job, tending bar at a small place in Westown, New York. She found a small bungalow for rent and made a lot of new friends. Robyn is that type of person, if you can't get along with her, you can't get along with God. That's why she was so much like her nanny, not a mean bone in her body, but don't shit on her. I missed her when she moved, but it was the best for her. She kept in touch with all her friends in Pearl River and was no stranger to picking up the phone and talking to her old man either. We were always close, even though the divorce with her Mother and she was smart enough to pick out the lies from the truth about me. There was nothing that Robyn and I could not talk about. There were no lies between us and that's the way it still is today.

Brian graduated from Delhi and took a job on a breeding farm in Andy's in upstate NY. He met a girl in college and got married and settled down on a small farm outside of town. The big house on Lark Street was empty with Brian and Robyn gone. It was the summer and Sue and I decided to move down to Oceanside, to her mothers. I would still work in Rockland County and come home on the week-ends and on Wednesday nights. It was about an hour's drive early in the morning to Rockland, but coming home on Friday nights it took me over two hours just to get across the Throgs Neck Bridge into Long Island. It was good, we were close to the boat that all of us enjoyed, and Loni had no trouble making the change in schools. She missed her big sister Robyn, but she made it up with her grandmother, who spoiled her rotten. I was staying with my buddy Jake, three nights a week, who had a small apartment next to the rail road tracks in Pearl River. Jake was like my buddy Jeff, we drank together and they both liked to come and watch Dixie and me play softball, and have a few beers after the games. This was the mid 1980s now, and softball playing was long gone for Frankie and me. Jake was, and still is my good friend. He is retired now, and moved back to his home town of Ogdensburg NY. on the Saint Lawrence River that separates the US and Canada. I know that he is safe there, his sisters and brother look in on him during the week and being seventy four years old, and he has a sixty year old girlfriend that's keeping him happy too. We call each other on our birthdays. That's what good friends do.

Shortly after moving to Long Island, I bought Sue a birthday present, a Golden Retriever puppy, nine weeks old. She was the runt of the litter. When I went to pick one out I noticed that one of the puppies was biting at my work shoe and untying my shoe lace. Well that was the one for me. She was tiny, but real cute and real blond. Both Sue and Mavis were dog lovers. Mavis had a Dauchsand of her own and this puppy would go over just fine. We call the puppy Liebchen, which means pretty girl in German, or Leaper for short. She was a good dog, and was easy to house train. She would go to the door when she wanted to go out and would wine or bark to come back in. She loved the boat and to ride in the car. All the girls were gone during the day. Loni was in school, Sue became a school bus driver and Mavis was a hair colorist in a hotel in New York City. The dog would not mess in the house. Mavis would take the train into the city and take it home at night. She always took the club car home where she could have a glass of sherry or two on the trip. If I was home from work during the week, I would go pick her up across from the train station at the Town House Bar, where we would have a drink, before going home. She was quite a gal, she was married once, it didn't last much after Sue was born and she had a boy friend, Babe for a long time but he wanted to get married and she wanted none of that. She was not going through that bull-shit again. She had her daughter and her granddaughter and her roses, she loved her rose garden and that was good enough for her. She had me too, her good friend, we really liked each other.

CHAPTER 22

Mavis was good at what she did for a living and had her own list of costumers that would make special appointments with her when they would come into the city. Some days she just wouldn't have to go into work and at other times she would stay in the city at her friend's house when she had late appointments. She would try to book herself out early on Fridays so that we could get an early jump for the weekend on the boat. She was a perfect partner, when it came to the boat. We lived with her about two years when one night and officer came to our door and told Sue that Mavis was dead. She had a late day at work, took the club car home and was on her way to the Town House Bar across the street and tripped on the stairs, leading down from the rail station, fell all the way to the bottom and broke her neck. Sue was beside herself. I stayed home with Loni while she went to identify her mother at the hospital morgue. I held Loni until Sue came home and then they both went into their rooms and cried their eyes out.

Mavis requested to be cremated with no viewing or big service. Sue notified all her friends and where she worked. She was very well liked and respected by her peers. Sue was left with all of her estate and requested that her ashes be spread along her rose bushes, which she loved so much. I did this for her, Sue couldn't bring herself to do it and I waited until there was nobody home, just me and Liebchen went outside and I spread them evenly. I was still working in Rockland County and was on a big job that was working every Saturday, not much time for the boat. We would go down on Sundays and take it out on day trips, but it wasn't the same without Mavis.

Sue told me that she wanted us to get married. She wanted medical benefits for her and Loni. She wanted to feel more secure than just living together. We got married and had a small reception at the club that I had worked part time in the winter lay-offs in East Rockaway NY. She also decided that she wanted to sell her mother's house and wanted to move to up-state NY, to get Loni into a good school system and a country atmosphere. It was ok by me, I was working there and it would mean less traveling and home every night. It was ok with me. Now, what to do with the boat? Well we decided to sell it and pay it off and pocket the profit, which wasn't much. We went looking for a house in Orange County NY. She found a big two story farm house on two acres of land. Sue fell in love with it right off the bat. She would take the money left over from Mavis's house, and her estate, to buy it.

During the time that we lived in Long Island, we bought a house in Hudson FL. I rented it out through a rental agent, one of my never to do mistakes again deals. Anyway this was the house that Sue and I would retire to when we were ready. It was a small, two bedroom home on a quiet street and the taxes were cheap. Well one thing after another went wrong with the house, the renter didn't pay the rent, and the septic system backed up and had to be replaced. They trashed the place when I had them evicted, then the rental agent went out of business with three months of my rent. What a horror show!! I was better off keeping the house vacant and just using it in the winter ourselves.

The house that we bought was in Middletown NY. Sue went back to driving a school bus. Loni was in high school by now and it was the best school system in the state. She was a good student, surprisingly for all the moving around we did while she was growing up, a very bright child. Sue and I were having marital problems and we separated. She left me and took Loni and went to the house in Florida and got a job tending bar. It seemed to me that after her mother passed away she just didn't know what the hell she wanted. It was like nothing would please her, me, her job, or anything. She was drinking and coming home late and just plain didn't give a shit about me or anything else. She just packed up and left me with the house that she had put her mother's money into and left. There I was, me and Liebchen, alone in the big house. The winter was coming on and I was getting ready to be laid-off from my job.

I thought that I had found the woman that I was going to spend the rest of my life with. Apparently I was wrong and it was just like my first marriage, it was going bad. After my first marriage, when Sue and I started living together we became the best of friends, we liked the same things, loved the boat and did everything together that couples in love do. When she pulled out and left me, I had lost my best friend, my mate.

It was time to start over again. Robyn was not living far away at this time and would come over and check on me and we would go down to where she was tending bar and have a few drinks. One Sunday I told her to come for dinner and I fixed one of her favorites, roast pork and mashed potatoes. It was good if I don't say so myself. The gravy was even good and I really don't know how to fix gravy. About one in the next morning I couldn't even get out of bed. I was balled up into a knot and couldn't stand up by myself. I got to the phone and called Robyn and she came right over and took me to the hospital. I had a gallbladder attack and needed an operation right away. I met the surgeon and wanted to put it off but he said that I could die and we needed to do it, like now! I said ok and away we went to the operating room. I was scared. I had been smoking heavy, was overweight and worried silly about Sue. I was a mess. Thank GOD for my pal Robyn, she had replaced mom, and saw me through, her and GOD. I woke up in a fog after the operation, in pain, but alive and grateful.

The next day I was still in a lot of pain. I woke up about seven in the morning and found Sue standing at my bed side. First I thought that I was dreaming, but she was there. Robyn must have called her, told her that I was having the operation and she and Loni drove all night to get here. I was surprised but didn't know what to make of it at the time. We talked and she said that she wanted to come home and for us to be together again. With all her faults, all I could remember was how great she had been with mom and how she took care of her while she was dying. That meant an awful lot to me. I loved her and I was torn up when she left me.

We sold the house in Florida and bought a small camping trailer and lot in Pennsylvania, to try and see if we could find something that we would enjoy together. It worked well at first, then Loni didn't want to go there, and Sue lost interest, so I thought. I was going by myself, there was fishing there and I liked that, plus it gave me a chance to get away by myself. It was only an hour from where we lived, not a bad drive at all. I came home early one Sunday afternoon from the camp site and found Loni and her boyfriend, Sue and a black man sitting at my dining room table. I was startled at first, and everybody started getting nervous. It didn't take me long to put two and two together. It looked like I was the odd person in my own house. What could I say, I was speechless. I started to shake with anger and had to get out of the house, before I killed someone, her or the black guy.

Now I knew why Sue didn't want to go to the camping trailer. She was fooling around with this guy for a while and the only person apparently that didn't know it was me. The heart was torn right out of me. I thought that when she came back that we were going to be fine. This was not to be, I was finished with the whole mess. I had to make a decision and that's what I did. I went and looked around for an apartment, found a nice small place over in Pine Island NY. I told Sue that I was leaving and she could have her house and all that went with it. She got mad and told me not to forget to take the dog with me, the puppy that I had given her for her birthday when we lived in Long Island.

I backed the truck up to the front door and started loading my things while she sat on the stair case watching me. I didn't say a word to her. She knew that this was the last draw for me, I would not share her with anybody, and as far as I was concerned she was dead to me. I took Liebchen, put her in the truck and we left. Two days after I moved out, her boyfriend moved into her house.

CHAPTER 23

Sue and I didn't see each other at all after I left her house. When I moved out I wanted to make sure that I didn't have to return there for anything. I lived in a small apartment over a bar in Pine Island. The place was called Victor's, he and his wife ran the place and they were nice to me. I paid my rent on time, stayed to myself, just me and my Golden Retriever. Liebchen was the best; she was a lot of company for me back then. She would lie at my feet at night while I was watching TV and when I went to bed, she was at the end of the bed. I could leave her alone during the day, while I went to work and she would wait for me to let her out, to do her thing, when I came home. I would let her run, the first thing every morning and she was good for the day. What a great dog she was.

During this time, I was fighting a bad case of depression; I was alone for the first time, in a long time. I had lost what I thought was my best friend and mate Sue. I felt betrayed and lost all at the same time. I would call my buddy Jeff when I was really down and he would pick me up the best he could and we would make plans for me to come down to Florida and see him on my winter layoff. He retired from the Army after over twenty years of service and settled there with his Mother and Aunt. His Father had died while he was away in the service and he wanted to be close to his Mom. He had been away for a long time.

We would talk for an hour or so. I really looked forward to our calls. I was working on a job in Rockland County again and I was commuting about an hour each way to work. The job was ending and it was just before Thanksgiving. Robyn and I had a Holliday dinner and I asked her if she could take care of Liebchen while I went to visit Uncle Jeff in Florida. I paid up my rent and took care of the dog with Robyn and I drove down to see Jeff. I had a good three weeks away, in the sun and I didn't want to come home to the cold and snow of December. I got home just before Christmas. The dog was glad to see me. I was glad that I went to Florida, I needed the break, to clear my mind and help get rid of this depression I was fighting. I had a lot of trouble getting Sue out of my mind. I was in sad shape, with a lot of crazy thoughts going through my head. Thoughts of ending it all and shit like that. I prayed for the LORD to help me, and I think he must have heard me. It was after the first of the NEW YEAR and I got a call from my friend and a business agent from the union.

He knew what I was going through with my marriage and knew that I was depressed. He told me that there was a job in Suffern, New York that needed trailer drivers and that he didn't have any out of work in the union hall. The job would go through the winter and that was fine with me. I would be busy and it would keep my mind off of other things. My Son Brian was working on the same job as a driver. He had left the horse breeding business after his first marriage ended and came to the union where I was working looking for work.

He was a good driver and was well liked and wanted to learn how to drive a tractor trailer. He had trained at this while he was on another job, and took the tests needed and got his trailer license. The only thing wrong with the job I was going to was that it was working at night. Six o'clock at night until midnight, five nights a week. It was good work, except when it snowed and you had to be careful on the frozen haul roads.

I had to get Liebchen retrained to the night shift and she didn't like it at first. I left the radio on while I was gone. I stayed on that job well into the spring and I found that the depression was leaving me and I was coming back to the real world. Just before leaving this job, I met this woman that a friend introduced me too. Her name was Ronnie, short for Verona, which she did not like at all. She was as Irish as patty's pig, a short red head with an attitude and the cutest smile in the world. We liked each other right away and started to date. This went on for about six months and then we decided that we should live together at her house in Monroe NY. I was on the re-bound and not ready to make the same mistakes that

I had made in my past two marriages. That's the last thing I needed. With Ronnie it was different; she was still married but separated for fifteen years. She was Catholic as was her daughter and didn't believe in divorce. She was not going to make her child a bastard child. The guy she was married to was a real asshole and even his daughter disliked him. He fooled around on Ronnie all the time and ended up having two children by another woman, which he lived with. Ronnie had no contact with him at all. She had her house and her little girl and she just kicked him out and that was that.

We got along great, she knew all about my problems and she was honest with me about hers. Her daughter liked me and her grandchildren liked me also. Helene was a great mother, she had six children and they would come to the house every Saturday morning to visit Ronnie. Ronnie was a lot like mom, not a mean bone in her, but lookout if you got her pissed off. The Irish would come out and then you were in trouble. The seven years we were together we never had a fight, not over anything. We had a special kind of love for each other, more like a great friendship for one another. We cried together and laughed together. We both liked the camper in Pennsylvania and would go there often during the summers. She enjoyed the trees and the quiet, and the fires we had in the outside fire place. She loved Liebchen and they became great friends. This was a good time in my life, I wasn't alone and we just seemed to flow into each other, like two rivers meeting, mixing into one. She was a great gal, mom would have liked Ronnie, and they must have been cut from the same cloth. My kids like her too and they were glad that

I found someone after I left Sue. Robyn was worried about me she could tell I was depressed, when Ronnie came along it all changed. We ended up good for each other, I knew that Ronnie was hurt bad when she caught her husband screwing around and I could relate to that too. Both of us had been in the same boat, we had trouble trusting someone again. The first year was like walking on egg shells. We took it slow and got use to one another. Once the trust was forged, with no lies and no bull-shit, we really got closer. She loved her grandchildren; they were the pride and joy of her life. Before I moved in with her I had to be divorced, this was easy because while I was living in Pine Island, Sue had me served with the papers and I had to get a lawyer. She said that we were not compatible. I guess that was at least true. I was also told that she had filed bankruptcy and that it was going to reflect on me. It certainly did, I had to get a letter stating that I didn't file bankruptcy and that we were separated when she did this. What a mess, I couldn't buy a car, get any credit cards, no loans of any kind for about five years. I had to carry that letter every time I needed credit, what bull-shit!!! Anyway we got divorced and Sue got part of my pension when I retired, about 7% each month. I was glad it was over and the hurt started to go away. Ronnie was working as an insurance claims person, she had a good job which she liked and she had a lot of friends there. Her one friend Bridgett, a nice Irish gal from the other side, rode to work together each day and would stop and have a drink before they went home. They were great pals, both Harps, both red heads. While living together I would go down to see my buddy Jeff. I was laid off most winters in construction and loved the Florida weather.

Ronnie didn't mind and we had talked about retiring down in Port Richey when the time came. Jeff and I would go to the American Legion, have a few beers and bull-shit with a few friends that I was making from my winter visits. We also went to a place called the Hutch, a little bar where a lot of golfers went on Fridays after they went out and embarrassed themselves on the course, it was a nice group of people and I made some friends there too. I looked forward to the winter trips, to see my best friend, and the rest of the crowed.

The following work year was very busy for me. I was finishing up a job and it was late September when Jeff called me. He told me that a friend of ours had to go into a nursing home and it looked like he wouldn't be getting out. He had sugar diabetes and they had to take one of his legs off and part of the other one. He informed me that our friend's condo was going to be for sale and he thought that it would be just right for me and Ronnie. He said that the price was right and for me to move on it quick. I would be buying the place sight on seen, but Jeff's word was good enough for me. He sent me up some pictures, it looked great, fully furnished and walk in condition. I talked it over with Ronnie and she said GO FOR IT. Jeff told me to send down a check for three thousand, ten % and he would go to his bank and get the ball rolling.

I got the mortgage on the condo and it only took four days for the closing to take place. Jeff did most of the running around for me and even lent me some money so I could get the deal. He told me that if I didn't buy it, he would. He had a big house all to himself since his mother and his aunt had passed away. He didn't need a three bedroom home and after he saw the size of my condo, he decided to sell his home and get a condo. He found one in great shape, two buildings away from mine. That was the best move he ever made, he is single, never married, and it's just a little smaller than mine. I made plans to come down that winter to see the place I had bought and spend three or four weeks there. I stayed five. Ronnie made plans to come down for two weeks, while I was there, she loved it. She bought a few little things for the place, dress it up a little. The people that owned it had no kids and the sister-in-law wanted a few personal things, from her sister, but that was it. She left it fully furnished and all I had to do was move in. Ronnie went home two weeks ahead of me. I was going to be unemployed until spring but I was informed that I was going to work on the biggest job coming out that year. The replacement of concrete decks of the Tappan Zee BRIDGE. This would take over two years and all the work would be done at night. That was the only drawback about the whole thing. We started the job in the spring. The bridge was on the New York State Thruway and the traffic, even at night was a bitch. Very dangerous to say the least, but the money was good.

CHAPTER 24

After my son's first marriage failed, he also returned to Pearl River, where he grew up and went to school. He had an apartment which he shared with another fellow and his younger sister Eileen. He was working fairly steady as a driver on a pretty big job. He did not get along with his younger sister and they had a parting of the waves, she left in haste and owing him a few months rent. They really don't talk much to each other to this day. It's too bad, but that's life, you can pick your friends, but not your family. This is where he met a nice gal, which became his second wife. They had a home in Pearl River for eight years, before going to the sunshine state. Before they moved to Florida, he and his wife would come to Monroe and visit Ronnie and me. They live about an hour and a half away from my condo in Florida, now. It seemed that we always lived close to one another. They got tired of the cold and the snow. Pearl River always seemed to draw us back.

My job on the bridge was shutting down for the winter months. Ronnie was not feeling well. She said that she had a bad cold; she was tired all the time and had a real bad cough. She went to the doctor; he wanted to take some tests at the hospital, on an outpatient basses. I took her there, they took blood and did a chest x-ray. She went to the doctor's office four days later to get the news. She came home with some medication and told me that it was a slight case of pneumonia, for her to get some rest and take the medications. She called into work and gave them the scoop, and said that she would be out for about two week, and would call her boss when she would be returning. That same week I took a fall on the stairs going to the basement to put some wood into our wood burning stove. I hurt my back and went to the doctor and he told me that I would have to get an MRI. I did, and the news wasn't very good. I had disc problems; two of them were pressing on a nerve and was giving me a lot of pain. I couldn't bend; walk straight up and when I woke up, it would take me ten minutes to get out of bed. Some days I had to walk with a cane. We were in bad shape Ronnie and I, both sick, both loused up. It was just before Thanksgiving and the Thruway would not let us work on the bridge during the holidays so we would close down from the end of November until the first week in March. It was the same shut down as last year. That gave me time to get my back fixed, I thought. The doctor operated on my back. I needed a partial disc-removal, which means that he had to shave the three disc that were pinching the nerve in my back and release the pressure.

With the pressure off the nerve the pain seemed to be gone. The surgeon told me that there may be some pain, but not like before. He also told me that my truck driving days were over. I could not be bouncing up and down on the truck seat or the dicks would continue to move back out towards the nerves and I would be in worse shape that I was when we started. He advised me to stop driving. Swell, what was I going to do, I was fifty nine years old, and trucking was all the work that I knew. He told me to think about retiring on a permanent disability and apply for my social security. I was out for the winter and thought that I had plenty of time to heal from the operation and I would go back to work in March.

It was after Christmas and I told Ronnie that I was going down to the condo for a few weeks. I wanted her to come with me, but she said that she didn't want to go. She still wasn't feeling good. I was worried about her but she just laughed it off and told me to go and see Jeff, she would be fine. She had gone back to work, but I think it was too soon, she seemed to be tired all the time. It wasn't like her; she blamed it on old age. I left for Florida; it was snowing that day and by the time I got to south Jersey the snow had stopped and there was no snow on the ground when I got into Delaware. Jeff was glad to see me and we talked about my operation and what the doctor told me to do. He agreed with the doctor and told me to go for it and retire if I could. I was only in Florida a week when I got a call from Ronnie asking me to come home. She was not well and didn't want to bother Helene. I knew it was not good news, if she didn't want to tell her daughter. She sounded very sick on the phone. I told her I was heading home right away, she said that she was sorry, that she loved me and to drive safe. I called Helene and told her what was going on and said that she would go over to her mother's house. I told Jeff that I was going and started the trip back to Monroe. I drove straight thru to New York, about thirteen hours; I stopped for an hours nap on RT.95 and then finished with a quart of coffee in hand.

When I got there, Helene met me at the door. Ronnie was in her recliner chair; she was very week and could hardly speak. Helene said that she spoke to her doctor and was told that he had told Ronnie that she had Cancer and that it was terminal and there was nothing to be done for her, he wanted her to go into a hospital, she was not doing that, she told him. If she was going to die, she would die at home. That sounded familiar, that's what mom wanted. Her daughter said that the doctor would call Hospice and have a nurse over on Monday morning and told her to increase her meds to make sure she would have no pain, we did this. It was Saturday night when I got home and Helene had been there since Friday afternoon. I told her to go home to her children and that I would take care of my friend. Ronnie was so week, she couldn't eat anything. I fixed her some chicken soup, her favorite, but she couldn't swallow. I got a little of it into her, not much. She would sleep for about two hours, and then be awake for a hour, that's the way it went most of the Saturday night. I got the pain medications into her through the soup.

It seemed to do the trick. She went off to sleep shortly after having the soup. This was the way it was all night and most of the next day, Sunday. I wanted to get her to eat, but all she would have was beef broth or more chicken soup. I was watching TV and I heard Ronnie moan and she looked at me and said three words, love you, and priest. I had been there with mom and knew that the end was soon. I called Helene and told her to bring her friend, her priest from her church. It was snowing hard that night. There was two feet on the ground and still coming down hard. It took them an hour to come six miles and they had to walk through snow drifts to get to the door of the house. When they came in the priest went to Ronnie right away and removed his cloth, she smiled at him, she knew. Helene told me to leave them alone, we went down stairs and I was crying. She was not, she knew that her mother was going to her GOD and she was ok with that, how strong she was. She was a devoted Catholic and trusted her GOD completely, loved her mother and knew that they would be together again someday. After a short time, the priest called down to us to come up and that my friend had passed. We said a prayer together and then we made the arrangements for Ronnie. The snow was very deep and we had to wait for the plows to come through for the funeral people to come for her. I was broken up; I had lost by good friend and companion. I was not happy that she had deceived me about her sickness, I would not have gone to the condo, and she knew this, and didn't want me to worry about her. She thought that she had more time to live. She was quite a lady and I loved her. Before the funeral people came, I bent over and kissed her on the forehead and said good bye and that I loved her too. Ronnie wanted to be cremated and that there wouldn't be a big service, they said a MASS for her and Helene took the ashes for an internment in the spring. Helene told me to stay in the house as long as I wanted. I told her thank you and that I would stay there for another month or so but I was going down to the condo as soon as I could get my affairs in order. There were too many good memories of Ronnie at the house and I just wanted to remember her, the way we were, and not the last two days of her life. I miss her still and think of her often.

CHAPTER 25

I stayed in the house for almost three months. During that time, the notice came that I was to get a permanent disability award from Social Security, and that my retirement was all set. I contacted the union pension office, told them the good news, and they informed me that I would start receiving my pension checks the following month. I then called Helene and told her that I was going down to Florida, for good and that I'm leaving at the end of the month, about two weeks. She was sorry about this but understood and wished me well. We still keep in touch to this day. She's like her mother, a great gal. I started making plans to leave. I gave my son a freezer for his boat club and a bedroom set to my youngest daughter Eileen. I was told to leave the set on her porch, which I did. Apparently she didn't want to meet me at her house to receive the furniture. I would have liked to have seen her before I left for the condo; I guess she didn't want it that way. Too bad!

I started to pack up my things and discard the stuff that I didn't want to take. It's amazing how much shit one person can save. I should know a lot about that, mom was a crap collector and I had to move her stuff from place to place through the years. I finally got it done the best I could. Now to get it all in my car, it was going to be a challenge. The car was loaded; there wasn't a square inch that didn't have something packed in it. The only open space of any kind was in the back seat, where Liebchen had to sit for the whole ride. I brought water and plenty of treats for her and when we stopped to eat she got a Mc Donald's burger too. She was great, not a problem the whole trip, she loved to ride in the car. I think she would have liked it better if there was a little more room though. We made the trip in two days and Jeff was glad to see us both. He looked at the car full of things and just shook his head in amazement. We got the car unloaded and Leaper had to check out the new territory. We weren't supposed to have large pets at the condo but there was no way that I was leaving without her. She was fifteen years old, didn't bark at all and was starting to have trouble getting up and down on her legs. She was completely house broken and she was staying and that was that. I took her to a vet down here and he told me that it wouldn't be long before she wouldn't be able to get up from a laying position. When that time came, bring her in to see him and he would give her a shot so that she could get up and move around better. She was my pal and I was going to do the best I could for her. A month after seeing the vet she could not get up from the floor. I carried her to the car and into his office. He told me that it was time to put her down. Her hips were gone and it was best to end her suffering. She looked up at me from the table she was on with a look in her eyes that told me that it was time for her to go. I broke down and the vet told me that I could wait in the other room while he gave her the shot. I told him that I was staying right there and I stroked her head as he inserted the needle and she closed her eyes and went to sleep. I had lost two of my best friends within six months. Once again I was a mess, but I had a lot of great memories with that dog, she had been a big part of my life and is still missed today. Losing a dog in your life, that you have loved for such a long time is like one of your family passing away and is hard to get over.

I got use to not having her around and lying at the foot of my chair and bed. I was lonely at times but keep myself busy. I had met another woman and dated her for a long time. I then found out that she was dating another man and that it was time for me to move on. I told you that I don't share. I'm greedy that way, you're either with me alone or you're not, pure and simple. I had made a lot of friends at one of the water holes, where I would go for a few beers and I met a great gal, her name is Kimmie and we found out that we liked the same things. She lived with her father, who was in his eighty's and she owns the house that they live in. We started dating and both wanted to take things slow.

We both liked to watch football on the TV. She went to THE Ohio State College and of course she is a big OHIO fan and so is her father. We were hitting it off very well and we also found out that we didn't like liars, or phonies. We had both had enough of that shit.

Kim is going to be fifty years old this year and is nineteen years my junior. I tell her that I'm a cradle robber. She's a hard working gal and takes real good care of me. She is not well, she has back trouble and fights pain every day. Some days are worst then others. She doesn't complain and just takes it in stride. I had become very careful when it came to women it seemed that I didn't have any luck in serious relationships for long periods of time. With Ronnie it was different, we were fond of each other, the love was there but there didn't seem to have the pressure of being married, or having one trying to change the other one. We could be ourselves, no lies and no phony feelings. This is the way it has been with Kim the past six years. My son and daughter have met Kimmie and they like her very much. Robyn knows that I'm taken care of and that I'm very happy. I know that Kimmie loves me very much, it is a feeling that I've felt before and quite frankly a feeling that I'm afraid of. Every time these feelings come along with a woman that I love, they end up leaving me one way or another. And I end up hurt and alone again. I had been through depression over a woman before and don't want those crazy thoughts coming back. I had Liebchen with me back then to help me, to take my mind off of things, but now I would be alone. Jeff would be there for me, like always, what a great friend he is. I don't think I have to worry, Kim seems pretty firm in her commitment to me and mine to her. We have lived together at the condo the past three years and it's worked out fine. Her dad still lives in their home about seven miles away and she goes over to fix his dinners for a few nights and freeze them, and set up his meds for the next week. He has a hard time walking and getting up from a sitting position. He uses a walker and takes it slow. He has a dog to keep him company and to bark when someone is on the property. He is eighty one and soon it will be time to get some help for him during the day on a steady basis. He is an old Marine and a hard ass, and doesn't think he needs anyone to take care of him. I don't know what he thinks Kimmie does, in taking care of him, but it's not just food, it's everything for him that he just doesn't see. He would be up shit creek if it wasn't for her. We won't tell him.

Chapter 26

Kim's Father is not doing very well at all, getting worse every day and we found ourselves going down to his house every day to fix things for him to eat and other things. During this period, I found out that my brother Frank was in Sloan Kettering Hospital in New York City. The seeds that he had put in three years before to combat prostate cancer didn't do the complete job of curing the disease.

The cancer started in the hip area and spread to his liver and other vital organs of his body. His wife, Michelle called me with the news and I knew that I had to get on a plane and go to see him. It was the early stages of being terminal and he could not walk or sit for long periods of time. I was glad that I went up to see him. We talked about the old days while he was in high school, in college and all the good times we had playing softball together. Memories that will never fade from my mind. I stayed in New York for ten days and then came back to Florida. He was supposed to be moved to a rehab center for while, and hopefully he would be able to go home and be with his family.

This was not to be. His condition became worse and he had to be moved to a hospital in New Jersey and was put into an intensive care unit there. He was in this unit over eight weeks, his wife by his bed side every day and his children would come in on a regular basis, day after day.

I was only home in Florida four weeks when I got the call that Frankie was moved to another hospital and that the doctors felt that the cancer had moved into his liver and that his kidneys had shut down. I was back on a plane, back north, to see my brother probably for the last time.

When I walked in the ICU of the hospital and saw him for that first time, I knew I had seen this look before. He was very pale, his skin was a light grey and his eyes were beginning to reset inwards. He was fading slowly. He was not fully conscience almost like a light sleep with his eyes open at times. I think that he recognized me when I spoke to him. I told him that I love him and that all his children loved him. I told him that it was okay to leave and go to be with Mommy and Dad. He loved life and was not going to give up easily. We both believe in God and knew that our faith in him was strong and that at the time of our death we will be reunited with our Mother and loved ones.

I stayed there eleven days but had to come home, I knew it would not be long before he would pass. His loving wife was by his side, every day refusing to let him give up, cheering him on until the end. The cancer finally won and his heart just could not keep up with everything else breaking down. Frank died on March 20, 2011. He was seventy five years old and was my hero in life and I will miss him greatly.

Just after I arrived home, Kim's Father took a bad fall and we took him to the hospital. This was not good, his legs were very bad, swollen and very red looking. He could not stand on his own and was bleeding internally and the doctors could not find out where he was losing the blood. He became very weak and started to fail rapidly. We all thought it would be best to move him to a hospice facility and that's what we did. He was awake and could talk to us. We took his best friend to see him, his little dog Tammy Sue; he was thrilled and full of smiles. We had made his day. It was great.

The day we took the dog to see Smokey, Kim's Father was the same day I got the call that my brother had died. We told Smokey about my brother and he told me that I had to go bury my brother up North taking Kim with me and if anything happed to him while we were gone, tell them to put him on ice and we would take care of him when we got home. Smoke was a Marine and so was my brother and that's what we did.

Kim and I were about to leave our home to go to the airport for my brothers funeral when we got a phone call from Hospice that Kim's Dad had just died while he was sleeping.

What a shock, it was expected, but not this soon or this quick. We went over to be with him and to set everything up. They were great and told us to go to New Jersey and bury Frank and we could take care of Smoke when we got home. I asked Kim if she wanted to stay home, but she would have none of it. She would be by my side all the way up North.

Needless to say, we had a quiet flight to New Jersey. It was a hard time for both of us. We had lost two loved one, two days apart from one another. Our love and our faith got us through.

We landed in New Jersey at Newark Airport around 8 o'clock at night. By the time we got our luggage and the rental car it was about 9PM. We got to our motel at 10PM and just fell down on the bed. This was a rough day for both of us and the worst was yet to come for me tomorrow. The viewing hours at the funeral home were 2PM to 5PM and 7PM to 9PM for the one day only. Well, this was amazing I was in awe of all the people that came to pay their respects to my brother. There must have been at least eight hundred people that came and passed his closed casket, praying and giving their condolences to Michelle and the three of Frank's children that were there. People just kept coming and coming, a line stretched out the door and into the parking lot. Many were town officials, police officers fellow teachers from Garfield High School as well as office staff from the school, came to pay their respects to their friend.

The viewing room was filled with flowers, over eighty arrangements of all different sizes and colors, mostly purple and yellow, the school colors. Harvey and Bill, his two best friends from his high school days came up from Florida to see their friend and to say goodbye.

Many of Frank's friends from Rockland and Bergen County's were there also. It was a long day for Michelle, the children, Kim and I. Tomorrow would start at 9AM at the funeral home.

Kim and I arrived early at the funeral home. I wanted a few moments alone with my brother before they took him to the church for a Mass. I knelt in front of his casket said my prayer and then I kissed his coffin and told him that I love him and that I would see him later on down the road. This was very hard for me, he was not only my brother, but he was also my good friend. He had some so called friends that deserted him many years ago, when he and his first wife divorced and this hurt him. His real friends did not do this; we stuck by him and helped him get through this hard period of his life.

Frank had a good life, he was well respected at his school where he taught, coached and was athletic director for over 51 years. Imagine the young minds that he influenced through all those years at Garfield. The young athletes that he helped to go on in life to become professional ball players and coaches. How many scholarships that he helped get for some kids that could not afford to go to college on their own? He loved his job, the kids in the school, the people he worked with and Garfield itself. His life was Garfield.

After the service at the funeral home they carried his casket into the hearse and loaded the multitude of flowers into a funeral truck and line up all the cars for the procession through the city to the church for the funeral Mass. After the Mass, Frank's casket was carried back into the hearse for the trip to the cemetery. The Garfield police department did a wonderful job holding up traffic at side streets for the line of cars, at least 80 that followed the hearse through the city to the Garfield High School, where out on the sidewalks, very quietly stood the entire student body, staff and teachers, their hands folded in prayer and many blessing themselves as my brother Frank's casket passed by.

It was amazing, at first I didn't realize what was happening. As we got closer to the school and I saw, my eyes filled with tears, all those kids saying goodbye to their coach. What a tribute to a really fine man and dedicated teacher.

We proceeded to the cemetery, his final resting place, where we all gathered into the front chapel room for the internment service. Two U. S. Marine Corp guards stood at each end of the flag draped casket. The priest, Michelle's cousin, said the internment service, which led to the two Marine guards to remove the American Flag from Frank's casket, folded it correctly and presented it to Michelle. This was the end of the service and the folks that came there, filed past Frank, placing single roses upon his casket and saying their farewells.

The family was the last to leave the chapel room. Kim and I preceded Michelle and Frank's children. As I went past his coffin, I bent over it once again, told him that I loved him and told him to save a place for me, next to him and mom in Heaven. Frank and Michelle decided to be buried next to each other in a mausoleum, in New Jersey and not in the family plot in New Hempstead, Spring Valley NY. This was their wish and I was fine with it. I knew in my heart wherever he was laid to rest, that he would be with mom. After the funeral was over, we gathered at a restaurant for a lunch, for close friends and family. It was a fitting affair, a good send off for a great guy. It was time for Kim and me to go home and make plans to bury her father, another Marine. We got back to the motel, packed our things, rested and got ready for our morning flight, back to Florida. I found myself weeping, remembering my child hood with Frank, and all the wonderful times we had together. I will miss him for a long time.

With all the unanswered questions there are in life, in the hard times that we go through such as these, we ask, why? Why did he have to go so early in life at age 75? He did so much for so many. A real good person, a great Father and a great Grandfather. We have to leave all the answers to God. Our trust and belief in Him will carry us through. I do not go to church on a regular basis, but I believe in God. It is with that belief in Him that will get me through this mourning period for Frank. He will leave a big hole in my life and I will miss our phone calls throughout the year, at birthdays, Christmas, Easter or just to say hello. We always ended our phone calls, telling each other that, I Love You.

I believe he is now with my "best-tis Pal" Mom.

The flight home to Florida was just as somber as the flight to New Jersey. My head was filled of thoughts of my brother and our growing up on Ridge Street in Pearl River. But now we had to go and make funeral arrangements for Smokey, Kim's father, who pass away just two days after Frank.

Jimmie D Stover or Smokey , as his friends and family called him, was born in Columbus Ohio , and was a big Ohio State football fan, a real [BUCK-EYE]. He was 81 years old when he passed away. Kim, her brother Ken, two grandsons, Shawn and Tim came in from different parts of the country to attend his funeral. Smokey was a Marine, like my brother Frank, and the Marine Corp Honor Guard from a local Detachment, performed a beautiful service, with the three volley gun salute and the folding of the American Flag. Our friend Gary, a state VFW Commander, was in charge of the service. His grandson Shawn said a few words and some funny stories about his grandfather. I said a few words about him, as well as his son Ken, with a few more stories. It was a fine service, Smokey would have liked it. He had been cremated and it was a memorial service at a funeral home. Kim and I will take his ashes back to Ohio, to intern them at his wife's grave site. Family and friends gathered afterwards for a small lunch, before going to their homes. Kim's brother and nephews, left a few days later, when their flights were due to leave.

Needless to say, March of 2011 was not a very good time for the Dawson and the Stover families. Life dose go on, and pain fades with time, but memories last forever, and Kim and I will always have them.

CHAPTER 28

As I reflect back through the wonderful years that I spent growing up in Pearl River, from Martin Place and on Ridge Street and when I returned to live on White Ave during my first marriage. The good memories, of going across the street to the back door of Mr. Ablondie's bar, for beer at the age of seven. Taking hot plates of food to my grandfather, to his room, in Mr. Spooner's big house next door. Collecting brown bottles for him, to put his special apple cider mix, into them. The talks we use to have while he smoked his pipe with that awful smelling Liberty tobacco, he put into it. The memories of my mother taking care of her brothers and her father when they had a snoot full of beer. The make-shift basketball court in the back yard that dad made for Frankie and the smell of the chicken coop when I went out to collect the eggs. I remember in the winter, the smell of mom burning the hairs off of plucked chickens that were going to be cooked sometime over the weekend. The windows of the house were closed during the winter and the smell would linger for days. The ashes we had to take out and spread in the driveway and the chicken pen. The wonderful cherry pies we had from the trees and the fresh vegetables that we got from the Spooners next door. This was great time in my life. The friends that I made, the school that I went to and of course my Mother and Father. Mom was the joy of my whole life, she was the rock that my brother Frankie and I built our lives around, the foundation that gave us the tools to go through life with pride and strength to handle the hard times that life throws at you. GOD knows that she had some of those hard times. She faced scrutiny from her mother-in-law early in her marriage with dad and refused to be intimidated, she took care of pop while he was dying and her brother Giggy when he passed away in the hospital. She had to bury them all, including my father. She was a strong woman and she endured all this in life because the most important thing in her life was her two sons and she was determined to be there for them while they were growing up. She stayed as long as she could with us, and then the GOD she loved took her in 1984.

It was a good time to grow up, not like it is today with all the drugs and people killing one another. Robbing stores and ripping off cars. People aren't polite either, they don't say good morning, hello, how are you. It's a shame, thank GOD I was brought up to do and say these things, to be nice to other people. I don't know what this world will be like in the future, the way kids dress and act, the crazy hair doo's.

This is sad. Some of the things that I have seen during my lifetime make me think that the LORD must have a great sense of humor.

My mother always taught Frank and me to respect other people, and our selves. To this day, we as brothers say that we love each other and hug and kiss each other when we meet, or say good bye. He is, and was an important part of my life while we were growing up. Now that we are in our senior years, he being seventy five and me being sixty nine years old, we really appreciate the wonderful years on Ridge Street. I wonder if other people that grew up in Pearl River feel the same as I do, about their street, the friends they made through the years, the effect that the town had on their lives, and what going to PEARL RIVER HIGH SCHOOL meant to them in later years. I saw the effect that it had on Frank, growing up just down the street from his athletic hero, Bruno Ablondi and being coached by his mentor Ira Shuttelworth. Ira's influence on Frank's life made him the teacher and high school coach that he became. I think that Frank was about to retire after fifty years of teaching and turn things over to his son Frank III who has also embarked on a teaching and coaching career. He had been ill as of late and realized that it was time to enjoy the rest of his life with his loving wife, his children, and wonderful grand children.

Many weeks have passed since the funerals of my Brother Frank and Kim's Father, Smoky. Kim and I now face the task of taking her Fathers ashes to be interned by his wife's grave in Columbus, Ohio. As I sit on my lawn chair outside of my Florida room, soaking up the warm Florida sunshine of a June morning I recall that our marriages, Frank's and mine were very similar and our lives as well. We both fell in love at an early age, he a freshman in college to a girl named Judy and me a junior in high school to a girl names Kathy, these were not the women that we were to marry. Our first marriages ended in divorce also. He had three children, a boy and two girls and I had the same. My children were about five years younger than his. His first marriage ended, as mine did not on very good terms but we both went on with our lives. He remarried and had another son and two more daughters and his new wife and their union lasted until his death, over forty one years. Tears swell up in my eyes as I think of these things. My second marriage only lasted three years, and we had no children. In the many conversations that we had together, Frank and I, we would share the same feelings about our kids. All our kids. We loved them all. His children, Deron, Kerry, and Kim moved far away when their Mother remarried and I know that he missed seeing them. This was very hard on him and we talked about this often.

I on the other hand was luckier than Frank, my kids stayed local and I got to see them quite often, maybe this is why I had a closer relationship with my kids, especially now that they are grown, and know that it's not easy to make a marriage or relationship work. Some people said that he and I were weak men because we didn't stay in our first marriage, that we found love, respect, and truth elsewhere. I say that's bullshit. All men are weak and a man that says he's not is a fool and kidding himself. Frank and I shared the same feelings when it came to dissolving our marriages. The truly hardest thing was leaving our children. This we would talk about many time, him, me, and our Mother. Anyone that thinks that this is being weak should as they say, walk a mile in my shoes. I have been in many relationships with different women and they all knew that my three kids were my life, bottom line. My brother Frank had three children from his first marriage, a son, Derron and two daughters Kerry and Kim, and from his second marriage to Michelle, another son Franklyn 111 and daughters Heidi and Joelle. He loved ALL his children very much, and all his grandchildren too.

I'm not a Grandfather yet and don't think that it is in my future. My children have decided not to have any kids and that's okay with me. Only one thing bothers me, I think that a person should be a Father or a Mother, a parent of some kind before they sit in judgment of other people. It's hard bringing up children staying in a loveless marriage and not putting your kids in a tug of war between Mother and Father at an early age. I thank God every night, when I pray that I had the Mother and Father I had. Brought me and Frank up the way they did, teaching us to treat people with respect and to forgive them for the weaknesses. Mom taught both of us well. I will think of Frank many times in the life I have left and remember him as a good man, a man that loved his wife, ALL his children and Grandchildren, a man who loved his job at Garfield High and me and my three kids also.

I will miss the phone calls we would make to each other on birthdays, and holidays, always ending with him saying, I Love You, kid.

Through all the pain of losing my Brother, I have also been blessed with a fine woman to share my pain. Kimmie has held me up when I have my weakest moments in mourning. I do the same for her when she has thoughts of her Father, Smokey, who dies two days after Frank. She has been a good woman in my life and I love her very much, a companion, a friend and lover that came into my life when I needed her most. We are good for and to each other and it has been that way for the past seven years. We pick each other's spirits up every day. She reminds me a lot of Mom. I truly think that she's a keeper and I hope to never hurt her in anyway.

I often wonder if Julius Braunsdorf knew or envisioned his town growing to what it has become today, and the influence that it has had on so many people. When he bought the land in the 1840's known as Muddy Brook, a swamp land, by the train tracks, to construct his factory a long side this brook on one side and the rail road tracks on the other side. When he started to lay out the roads of "his town" and when in 1872 Dr. Ves Bogart found some pearls in small mussels in the Muddy Brook and the town's name was changed forever to Pearl River.

The town has a great history, from its founder, to the business's that help build it , to some of the famous people that came from it. I think that Mr. Braunsdorf is proud of what it has become. I know that I for one can say that I am proud to have grown up in Pearl River, with my brother Frank, my father Frank Sr. and of course my "best-test pal' MOM!!! I'll always love you.

END